THE MIDDLE AMERICANS

An Atlantic Monthly Press Book

Little, Brown and Company

Boston · Toronto

THE MIDDLE AMERICANS
PROUD AND UNCERTAIN

TEXT BY ROBERT COLES
PHOTOGRAPHS BY JON ERIKSON

We dedicate this book to the people who appear or speak on these pages, and to the millions of others like them — all of whom have the right to be heard and understood and, not least, represented and governed by men who labor hard to bring out the best in each one of us.

ATLANTIC—LITTLE, BROWN BOOKS
ARE PUBLISHED BY
LITTLE, BROWN AND COMPANY
IN ASSOCIATION WITH
THE ATLANTIC MONTHLY PRESS

Published simultaneously in Canada
by Little, Brown & Company (Canada) Limited

PRINTED IN THE UNITED STATES OF AMERICA

PREFACE

In this book we hope to bring before the reader something about the lives of millions of American citizens, perhaps a numerical majority of the nation's people. Men and women like the ones we have pictured and written about and encouraged to speak do *not* call themselves "silent Americans" or members of the "white, lower middle class" or elements in a so-called "backlash." Nor did we think of them in those terms when the work of this book was begun five years ago; the words were not then in widespread use. No, these men and women both proudly (and at times nervously) call themselves "plain people" or "ordinary people" or "average people." In their own way they put themselves through the same kind of classification their anxious, meticulous, wordy, label-prone observers attempt. That is to say, in the course of their plain, ordinary, average lives they make decisions about what they believe and want out of life, and wish for their children and their neighborhood and indeed, their nation. Often enough, too, they decide who they are *not,* perhaps do so rather defiantly and persistently: they are not black, not red, not brown, not unemployed, not eligible for or desirous of welfare, not intellectuals, not hippies, not members of a drug scene, a youth cult, a "counterculture," not in general against our military position in the world, not rich, not professional men, not "big businessmen," not individuals exceptionally well-born, well-to-do, well-educated — well able to influence their communities this or that way. Their views may coincide with those of conservative bankers, or lawyers, or members of the so-called "black bourgeoisie," or for that matter, with various kinds of student activists or liberals or even radicals, but their views are theirs, and have to do with their particular experiences and values and hopes and resentments and fears.

Nor do we mean here to offer a "scientific sample" of exactly what so very many American people believe. No "representative populations" have been selected; no questionnaires have been handed out. We make no claim to know what so-and-so many people think about one or another subject. No percentages are offered here; nor are there any "data" to be analyzed and proclaimed. Nor do we have a social and political theory to offer — that there is some "new majority" or "new politics" or "emerging voice" in America. We wish to make it quite clear that we look upon ourselves as observers, that alone. Our task has been to see and hear, in

v

so far as we could, how certain families live, families headed by men who are policemen, firemen, factory workers, bank tellers or lower-level bank officers, schoolteachers, telephone repairmen, construction workers, clerks and typists and small farmers and small storekeepers and on and on. Our task here is not to criticize these people, argue with them, praise them as America's answer to anything and everything, or use them as a means of advancing certain values or purposes we happen to have. And, anyway, who *are* "they"? Which people, indeed, go up to make "them"? What, indeed, do "all those people" believe? We feel that these are questions easier asked than answered; in fact we have heard so much said by all the men and women we have met and watched and spoken with that we marvel at the way some political leaders or social scientists find it possible to speak so decisively and unequivocally about the various wishes and loyalties of perhaps a hundred million Americans.

Still, the people here are, again, not students or out of work or blacks or rich or members of law firms or medical societies; and such facts do define them somewhat, not only in their own minds, but in relationship to others in the United States. As I move from home to home I do hear certain themes come up, certain faiths affirmed, certain antagonisms expressed — all of which I have tried to indicate by drawing upon years of taped interviews with dozens of families. I started working with those families in 1965. I had for a long time been living in the South, where I studied the way both white and black children came to terms with school desegregation. As a result of that work I became more broadly interested in the different kinds of families that are to be found in various sections of this nation. When I was taking my training in child psychiatry I mostly came to know upper middle class children and their parents. When I lived in Mississippi and Georgia I began to work with children whose parents were share-croppers or tenant farmers or migrant workers. For a while I worked in Appalachia with children who grow up in the hollows of eastern Kentucky or West Virginia. Most recently I have tried to understand how black children manage when they are bussed from a ghetto to suburban neighborhoods where only white children live; and it was in the course of such work that I first started visiting the homes of workers sometimes described as blue-collar or white-collar — whose children have for the first time found themselves at school with boys and girls often enough collectively called "them."

As with my work in the South, what started out to be a specific study of children under social stress became a more general effort to look at how particular families get along and come to terms with the various pressures that life eventually imposes. In Volume One of *Children of Crisis*, subtitled *A Study in Courage and Fear*, I describe at length the work I do — work which has required me to become a social anthropologist of sorts, even as I continue to be a physician and a child psychiatrist. In the second and third volumes of *Children of Crisis* (the subtitles tell about the work: *Migrants, Sharecroppers, Mountaineers* and *The South Goes North*) I will continue a more formal and extended presentation and discussion of my research, but I think it fair to say right here that in recent years nothing has taken more of my time and energy than the meetings I have had with some of the families described in this book — families I have gone once, sometimes twice a week to visit.

In those visits an hour can become an afternoon or an evening. In those visits one sits and talks and watches television and in general becomes a regular guest, a friend — but still, the doctor who has something on his mind to ask about, however indirectly he goes about doing so. In those visits one like me, trained in hospitals and clinics, is always looking for the strains, the troubles, the fears and worries — whereas, of course, the people I see are not patients, are not "sick," and, like everyone, go along from day to day, trying to make the best of their lives.

If my words help clarify how such people come to psychological terms with the particular set of social and economic circumstances that characterize their everyday existence, then the photographs taken show something else, something broader and more comprehensive, something about the *lives* of certain American citizens in the twentieth century. Jon Erikson has for years worked alongside people not unlike the ones he has now photographed. Again, in the tradition of social anthropology, these photographs represent well over a year of study — and, of course, travel over the length and breadth of a large and complicated nation. Jon Erikson has on his own met and come to know people, and taken his pictures. I have been doing my work alone. He has never met the families I work with, nor did I ever accompany him on any of his photographic expeditions. The pictures have their own integrity, their own narrative to tell, as do the people who speak, whose lives are in one sense being "studied" (hopefully not in a way that is condescending, insulting, demeaning or abusive, as certainly can be the case in this nation of "research projects"). Yet, Jon Erikson and I have shared our thoughts and ideas with each other, and struggled to give this book a certain coherence that has to do with our own conviction that there are indeed certain shared assumptions among the people the reader is about to look at and read about. We aim to convey those assumptions, convey them in the quiet but commanding and evocative (and provocative) way that photographers can, and convey them in the direct and outspoken (and also, implied, concealed and barely discernible) ways that people do when they talk and thereby make themselves heard. No doubt there are repetitions, currents and cross-currents in the book, and hopefully they are instructive. The photographs show lives being lived out; the words spoken by various men and women show something of what is going on "inside" them — a little, and sometimes *only* a little "below the surface." I believe that in this book the text and photographs are especially complementary. As I look at the photographs I am reminded that the people I sometimes hear speak so intensely or grimly or fearfully are also people who work, play, laugh and do a hundred things they never talk about or even think of mentioning. As I read the words I am reminded that the people Mr. Erikson has watched so carefully and captured in such a wide variety of activities are also people who have moments when they think long and hard about their country and their neighborhood — and ache to talk about what they think.

It is our belief that observers like us have a responsibility to be as fair and honest as possible; which means, not try to edit remarks to suit our ideological convictions, our political beliefs, not make these men and women and children caricatures of themselves, and finally, not become apologists for them, advocates of one or another of their views, or sly enemies dressed up as observers. In June of 1966, I wrote for the *Atlantic Monthly* "The White Northerner." The article's purpose was directly and urgently stated: to point out how many Americans feel left out, confused, ignored, enraged, needy in ways perhaps not at that time too obvious. Certainly since then the "problem" posed by such people and their "attitudes" has become thoroughly obvious indeed. Yet, we have worked on this book for a long, long time, and not, we believe, out of faddish compliance to a given "moment" in history. They are long-standing and difficult issues, the ones to which the people who appear in this book address themselves; they are issues that have a history, and they are issues that deserve to be examined, analyzed and, hopefully, worked on. No one will be helped by a spate of rhetoric which uses one group of Americans against another, or selectively pinpoints one set of views held by millions of people — as if all of us don't, time and again, have to contend with our doubts, misgivings, self-declared contradictions and almost acknowledged perplexity. If certain politicians often do just that kind of mischief, the rest of us have to be all the more on guard.

We particularly hope that so-called liberals will not, in their rush to understand yet another "problem," indulge themselves in endlessly hysterical and foreboding conclusions about the very same people whom, from the other direction, conservatives are likely to see excitedly and not always with reason as their new-found allies and saviors. If anything, the self-described "ordinary" people of this nation feel caught enough "in-between," feel in the middle of enough conflicts. The sudden interest they now are receiving from all directions may be yet another and ironic instance of that same predicament: they may prove to be everybody's foil or excuse or cause — and still feel without the persisting sense of themselves, the confidence and assurance about things, about the future, that go to make people reasonably (and it can only be that much) satisfied with their lot.

In any event, we will not demean these "proud and uncertain" people (or ourselves) with a declaration of our "concern" for them, or our respect and affection for them. We have learned a lot from them, seen and heard and been made to think a lot — about ourselves as well as them. In that sense we feel the debt any student owes to a concerned and patient and generous teacher. And we have put together this book because we believe that elsewhere there are more than a few like us, people badly in need of being asked by good teachers to stop and look and listen and think.

Again and again we have been compelled to realize how various — wonderfully so, confusingly so — the human beings we here call "middle Americans" can turn out to be. I realize that at times in this text I struggle vainly to suggest that variety. As one goes from home to home one reaches desperately for more nouns, more adjectives, more modifying phrases — in the perhaps futile hope that what James Agee called "human actuality" somehow will come across. In a way I hope those "modifiers" occasionally do indeed stop the reader, cause him to think about the value of catch-all categories, even ones used here for that sad reason, "convenience." Also for convenience, and to offer a certain direction for the eyes, Jon Erikson has arranged his photographs so that they move along from working people to their homes and families, their activities and involvements and associations — and finally to their predecessors and followers, the young who soon will (hopefully) be on the job, and the old who have done their fair share of work.

THE MIDDLE AMERICANS

I

"WE ARE PROUD OF OURSELVES, that's what I'd like to say. We're not sure of things, though; we're uncertain, I'm afraid, and when you're like that — worried, it is — then you're going to lose a little respect for yourself. You're not so proud anymore." There he goes, like a roller coaster; he is up one minute, full of self-confidence and glad that he is himself and no one else, and the next minute he is down, enough so to wish he somehow could have another chance at his life, start in again and avoid the mistakes and seize the opportunities and by God, "get up there."

Now, where is "there" for him? In the observer's mind the question is naturally asked, but the man who speaks like that about his destination would not understand why anyone would feel the need to do so, require a person to say the most obvious things in the world. In fact, if the question were actually asked, the man would have one of his own in return, which out of courtesy he might keep to himself: you mean you don't know? And that would be as far as the man would want to take the discussion. He has no interest in talking about life's "meanings," about his "goals" and his "values." At least, he has no interest in a direct and explicitly acknowledged discussion of that kind. He feels more comfortable when he slides into such matters, when he is talking about something quite concrete and of immediate concern and then for a few minutes finds himself "going off." It is not that he minds becoming introspective or philosophical or whatever; he likes to catch himself "getting carried away" with ideas and observations. What he dislikes is the self-consciousness and self-congratulation and self-display that go with "discussions." Perhaps he is "defensive" about his lack of a college education. Perhaps he feels "inferior," suffers from a poor "self-image." Sometimes a visitor slides into that way of looking at a person, even as sometimes the person being branded and pinioned comes up with considerably more than the self-justifications he at first seems intent upon offering: "Maybe we should ask ourselves more questions, Doris and me, like you do. I don't have time for questions; and neither does my wife. Mind you, I'm not objecting to yours. They're not bad questions. I'll have to admit, there'll be a few seconds here and there when I'll put them to myself. I'll say, Joe, what's it all about, and why in hell kill yourself at two jobs? I'll ask myself what I want out of life. My dad, he'd do the same, I can remember."

3

He can indeed remember. At forty-three he can remember the thirties, remember his father's vain efforts to find work. He can remember those three letters, WPA; he can remember being punished, shouted at, and grabbed and shouted at some more, because he dropped an ice-cream cone. Did he know what a nickel meant, or a dime? Did he know how few of them there are, how hard they are to come by? Now, his youngest son has a toolbox, and once in a while tries to pound a nail through a nickel or a dime, or even a quarter. The father gets a little nervous about such activities, but soon his apprehension gives way to those memories—to an amused, relaxed moment of recall. Indeed, it is just such ironies, both personal and historic, that get him going. And that is how he often does get going, with an ironic disclaimer: "I don't want to go on and on about the depression. My dad will do that at the drop of a hat. We've never had another one so bad since the Second World War started, so I don't believe we're in danger. But you can't forget, even if you were only a kid then. When my kids start complaining, I tell them they should know what their grandfather went through. I start telling them what it was like in America then; but they don't take in what you say. They listen, don't get me wrong. No child of mine is going to walk away from me when I'm talking. I have them looking right at me. But they think I'm exaggerating. I know they do. My wife says it's because they were born in good times, and that's all they've ever known. Maybe she's right. But even now for the workingman, the average guy, it's no picnic. That's what I really want my kids to know: it's no picnic. Life, it's tough. You have to work and work and work."

Then he adds that he likes work. No, he *loves* work. What would he do without it? He'd be sitting around. He'd go crazy. He'd last maybe a few weeks, then go back and be glad to be back. True, he'd like to get rid of his second job. That's not work, what he does in the evenings — after supper, or on weekends and some holidays. He needs the extra money. The bills have mounted and mounted. Prices are not merely "up"; they are "so high it's a joke, the kind of joke that makes you want to cry." So, he finds "odd jobs," one after the other, but when he talks about them he doesn't talk about his *work;* he refers to the *jobs,* and often enough, the damned jobs.

He can even be heard talking about the "slave time" he spends, and his mind is as quick as anyone else's to pursue that particular image: "You've got to keep ahead of the game, or you drown. The more money you make, the more you spend it, even if you're careful with money; and we are. We've so far kept up, but it's hard. I get odd jobs. I'll work around the clock sometimes, with just a few hours off to nap. I wire a building. I can do plastering and painting. I'm a steam fitter, but I'm handy at anything. A man wants some work on his house and he gets me to do it. He doesn't want to pay high union wages and doesn't want to register every change he makes in his house with the city officials, who'll make him lose his shirt

4

doing unnecessary things — or paying them off. If he could do the work himself, like I can, he wouldn't hire anyone — because he's in the same tight squeeze I'm in, we're all in. But he's a schoolteacher, you see, or he works in an office, and he can't do anything with his hands, so I get the work. I feel bad taking the money from them, I mean it. But I do the job good, real good, and I've got to have the extra money. I get a good salary every week. We live in a real good house. We live as comfortably as anyone could ever want. I work for one of the biggest real estate companies in the city. They keep me going. I'll be in one building, then I move on to the next one. I put in heating systems, fix boilers. I do everything. In the winter there's emergencies, a pipe has frozen, you know. In the summer we get ready for the winter. Even so, with good wages, we can barely keep our heads up over the water. Doris and I, we go wild with those bills. I tell her we've got to stop buying everything. Once I said we're going into the woods and live in a tent and hunt our food and grow it. She said that was fine with her, and I had no argument. So, I laughed; and she did, too.

"No, I guess we're where we are and we have to stay here, and so long as I've got my health, my strength, we'll do all right; we'll get by. The niggers are moving toward us, you know. They're getting big ideas for themselves. I hear they're making more money than ever before. They're pushing on us in the unions. They want to be taken in fast, regardless of what they know. A man in the trades, he's got to prove himself. You can't learn to be a good steam fitter or electrician overnight. But they're pushing for quickie jobs, that's what. I say to hell with them. Let them take their turn, like everyone else. That's another reason to make more money on the side. If we ever had to leave here, because they started coming in, then we could. There are times when I feel like a nigger myself; I'll admit it. I've been going all day, and I'm back at work after supper, and I'll be sweating it with a pipe or a radiator, and I'll say to myself: Joe, you're a goddamn slave, that's what you are; you might as well be picking cotton or something like that. And my face is black, too, from the dirt in the cellar!"

He smiles and moves toward a cup of coffee nearby. He stretches himself on a leather chair, the kind that unfolds in response to the body's willful selective pressure and has the occupant no longer sitting but lying back, "in the perfect position for television." He watches television when he can, and if he were home more he would watch more television. He likes to view sports — football, basketball, hockey. He will watch golf, but not very enthusiastically. He has never played golf. The game is too slow for him, and there is, too, a touch of the fancy in those clubs and the carts and the caps a lot of golfers wear. So he thinks, anyway; and he knows why. His father used to tell him that golf was a rich man's game. He now knows better; even his father knows better. But knowing is not being convinced. In his words: "You can know something, but you can't change

5

the way you feel." (So much for whole textbooks of psychology and psychiatry.)

As a matter of fact, the game of golf can prompt him to reflect. He has a friend who plays golf. The city golf course is crowded, though. In order really to enjoy the game one must belong to a club, have access to a first-rate, uncrowded course. The friend has a friend — his lawyer, in fact — who takes him to a fine country club. Every Saturday morning the two men play golf, then go home and meet again the next Saturday. They don't have lunch afterwards, or breakfast beforehand. They don't talk much to each other. What they have in common is golf, period. And there is a lesson in that. It's hard to "move away from your own kind of people."

Joe and Doris see no reason to make lists of "criteria" that characterize the people they feel comfortable with, or on the contrary don't; but upon occasion they will spell things out rather clearly. Joe will talk about "brainy people." One of his friends has a son who is just studying and studying, not in order to become a doctor or a lawyer (which is fine) but to stay out of the draft (Joe thinks) and "because he's so shy he can't talk to people, so he lives in the library." The subject of libraries and the universities that own them leads to other matters. Joe and Doris want those libraries and universities for their children, and indeed, their oldest son is in his first year of college. But no one can be snobbier, more arrogant and condescending than "a certain kind of professor" or a lot of those "professional students," which means students who are not content to study and to learn, but make nuisances of themselves, flaunt themselves before the public, disrupt things, behave like fools. He gets angry as he gets further into the discussion, but his wife slows him down, and even manages to cause a partial reversal of his views. After all, she insists, he is always complaining about certain things that are wrong with the country. He is always saying that the rich are getting richer, and the ordinary man, he can barely keep up with himself. Someone has to do more than complain; someone has to say unpopular things. Doris herself does so, says unpopular things, at least at certain times — though only to her husband, when they are having a talk. And soon Joe switches, says maybe, says yes, says it is true that some of the students are good, mean well, are on the workingman's side against the big corporations.

They don't like those big corporations; Joe and Doris don't, and their neighbors don't. If the students are at different times called vulgar, wild, crazy, insulting, and obscene, the corporations are declared clever, wily, treacherous, dishonest, and powerful beyond belief. Doris believes in "balancing things," and she believes in keeping her cool. She wants her husband, also, to have a certain distance on events. When he takes after college students, she reminds him that they have one in the family, hope to have more in the family as the years go by. And she brings up the corporations, and the way they "behave." They are decorous and restrained, but in Doris's mind they are no less outrageous than "the bad element" among the stu-

6

dents, the ones who "look so awful" and make her and everyone she knows feel uncomfortable and puzzled and really, at a loss.

After a while one can see that Doris and Joe are just that: at a loss to figure certain things out, at a loss to know how their own various opinions can ever become reconciled into some consistent, believable and coherent viewpoint. To some extent, they well know, the task is hopeless, because like the proudest, most knowing social critic, they are thoroughly aware of the ambiguities and ironies they, we, everyone must face: "I try to slow Joe down. He'll be watching the news, and he shouts at the demonstrators, you know. He doesn't like the colored very much. He says they're pushing too hard on the rest of us. I agree, but I think we ought to be careful, because the children will hear, and they'll repeat what they listen to us saying in Sunday School, and that's no good. Our son wants to be an engineer. He is in college. He is a sensible boy. He'll never be a radical or a militant. But he tells his father to go easy, and I agree. Where I go wild is on prices. They go up and up and no one seems to want to stop them. I voted Republican for the first time last year, because I thought they'd do something. But they're like the Democrats. They're all the same. They're all a bunch of politicians, every one of them. Joe says I'm as nutty when I talk about politicians and the prices in the supermarket as he is when he talks about the colored and the college students.

"There are times when I wonder who really runs this country. It's not people like us, that I know. We vote, we do what we're supposed to do and we go fight in the wars — I lost a brother in the Second World War and a cousin in the Korean War, and I hope to God my son doesn't end up in Vietnam, like my nephew, his cousin — but we don't get any place for being good citizens. There are some big people, in Washington I guess, and they make all the decisions; and then it's left for us to go and send our boys to fight, and try to pay the high prices that the politicians have caused us to have. Don't ask me more. I don't know who the big people are. But it's a clique. They own the stocks in the banks and the corporations. It's up to them, what the country does. We get these letters from our congressman, that he sends around, and it's just a lot of talk. Why, even my thirteen-year-old daughter knows better. She read the newsletter and she said he was just talking out of both sides of his mouth. Well, I went up and hugged and kissed her. I put my name on a list at the supermarket, protesting high prices. I guess that's how he got my name in the first place, that congressman. To tell the truth, I don't remember his name, and I don't want to."

Not that she or her husband spend much time talking about such frustrating, mystifying and upsetting issues. By and large they shun what Doris calls "current events." There is more than enough to do from day to day. Joe works almost all the time. Doris does, too. She has four children to look after. She has a house to keep clean, very clean. She has her aged mother to visit, who lives nearby with Doris's older sister. And then of late

7

Doris has also had to find work. She doesn't "always" work, but she "helps out" at a luncheonette for two hours, eleven to one, five days a week. Her husband did not want her to do so, but she insisted, and she got her way. She rather likes the work, serving the crowded tables. She gets a view of the outside world. She meets people. She hears people talk, and she learns what is on their minds. She makes a few dollars. She feels more independent. She feels that time goes by more quickly. And much as she dislikes talking about all the world's problems, she finds herself listening rather intently to what others have to say about those problems: "I can't help it. I'll be coming over to a table with the food, and serving it, and I'll hear them, the men on their lunch hour, and the women, too. They all talk the same way, when you come right down to it. They're worried about where the country is going. Yesterday I waited on a man who lost his son in Vietnam. You know how I know? I heard him telling his friend that the boy died so we could be safe over here. I'm sure he's right. I couldn't help wondering what I'd say if it happened to me, if I lost my son. I guess I'd say what he did, that man. My husband says there's nothing else you *can* say. You have to believe your own government. I mean, if you start turning on your own country, then what have you got left? The answer is nothing, I guess.

"I don't think the country is being run the way it should be. Don't ask me how I'd do better, but everyone I know agrees we're in trouble: boys dying every day over there in the jungle, and here the criminals taking over. There's the big gangsters, the Mafia, and there's the demonstrators, and downtown there's the colored — little boys, no more than ten or twelve a lot of them, looking for things to steal. I've seen them steal in the department stores. They knock down women and run away with their pocketbooks. I don't even carry one any more when I go shopping in town. And I only go there to do holiday shopping, because most of the stores have branches out in our plaza. Why don't the students and the college people demonstrate against the criminals? My sister-in-law was knocked down by three colored boys. They had a knife! They said they'd kill her. They took her pocketbook and ran. And you hear the Negro people asking for more, more, more!"

She would go so far and no further. She would never use the word "nigger." Her husband does, all the time he does; but when he goes further, starts cussing and swearing, starts sending people to hell, starts making sweeping, utterly unqualified judgments, she tries to stop him, and usually manages to succeed. She even gets him to reverse himself somewhat — which means, she gets him to say a number of *other* things he believes. For example, he believes that at birth "we're all just about the same," and he believes "it's the education a child gets that makes the difference," and he believes that "if a child is born poor and he doesn't get good food, then he's going to pay for it later."

8

As a matter of fact when he is feeling reflective and not pushed into a liberal corner by anyone, Joe will come up with some rather strong-minded rebuttals of his own assertions: "I can see how the niggers feel cheated out of things. If I was a Negro, I'd be madder than hell. I'd stand up to anyone who tried to keep me away from my share. We have a couple of them, carpenters, working with us on the job now. They're the best guys you could want. They work hard, and they're smart. They speak good, as good as anyone I know. If all the Negro people were like those two, then I can't believe we'd be having the trouble we are. A man is a man, that's what I believe; I don't care what his skin color is, or where he goes to church. This country has every kind of people in it; and it's all to the good, because that way no one group runs the show. The thing that bothers me about the Negro people is this: they're not like the rest of us, and I don't mean because their skin is a different color. I drive through their neighborhood. I've worked in the buildings where they live. I've listened to them talking, when they didn't even know I was listening. I'd be working on the pipes and I'd hear them from another apartment or down in the cellar. (The sound carries!) If you ask me, they're slow, that's what I think. They're out for a good time. They want things made easy for them — maybe not all of them, but plenty of them. They actually want relief. They think they're entitled to it!"

He stops. He lifts his head up, ever so slightly but noticeably nevertheless, and significantly. He is about to reminisce. After several years of visiting his home and getting to know him and his family, one can anticipate at least that much, the several directions his mind will pursue, if not the particular message he will deliver on a given day. So, he takes a slightly longer swallow of beer, and waits a few seconds, as if to pull them all together, all his memories. And then he is on his way: "I remember my father, how it killed him to take money from the government, the WPA, you know. I remember him crying. He said he wished he was never born, because it's not right that a man shouldn't be able to earn a living for his family. He could have stayed on relief longer, but he got off as fast as he could. He hated every day he didn't work. I guess they made some work for people, the WPA did; but no one was fooled, because it was phony work. When a man really wants to do something, and instead he's raking leaves and like that, he's even worse off than sitting on his porch all day — except that without the money, I guess we all would have starved to death.

"Now with the niggers it's different. They want all they can get — for free. They don't really like to work. They do work, a lot of them, I know. But it's against their wish, I believe. They seem to have the idea that they're entitled to something from the rest of us. That's the big thing with them: they've suffered, and we should cry our heads off and give them the country, lock, stock and barrel, because we've been bad to them, white people were. I have friends, a lot of them; and let me tell you, not one of them goes along

9

with that way of thinking. You know why? It's an insult, it's an insult to you and me and everyone, including the niggers themselves. If I was a Negro, and someone came up to me and told me how sorry he was — sorry for what he'd done, his people had, and sorry for the Negro people — I'd tell him to get away fast, real fast, if he wanted to keep his good health. Pity is for the weak; my grandfather used to tell us kids that. But your niggers, a lot of them want pity; and they get it. You know who gives it to them? The rich ones out in the fancy suburbs, they're the ones — the bleeding hearts, always ready to pat people on the head and say you're wonderful, and we love you, and just sit back, we'll take care of you, with welfare and the rest, just like we do with our pet dogs."

There is more, much more. He fires himself up as he gets deeper and deeper into the subject, the issue, the argument he is setting forth. He reaches for more beer, and his wife gets slightly worried, then obviously nervous, then somewhat alarmed. She wants him to stop. She wants us to change the subject. She doesn't necessarily disagree with the thrust of his remarks; but the more he speaks, the longer the exposition, the more explicit the references and criticisms and illustrative examples, the more uncomfortable she feels. Why? What bothers her about her husband's ideas? He asks her that. She has told him that he is getting "carried away." He says yes, he is getting carried away with the truth, and if that is wrong, it is also rare "in this country, today." He invokes the "credibility gap." He reminds us that politicians and businessmen tell lies all the time. He insists that "a lot of very proper types" delude themselves and fool others. It is hard to be honest, and for that reason most of us shirk saying what we know "in our hearts" is true. People are afraid to speak out, say certain things, because they know they'll be called "prejudiced," and in fact they are not at all that; rather they are "letting the chips fall where they do."

But yes, he goes on to acknowledge, she is right, his wife; she always is, as a matter of fact. What is the point of working oneself up into a virtual frenzy over people who themselves never let anything really trouble them? In his own words and manner he says that he actually rather accepts his wife's disapproval — and anticipates exactly why she "really" was made anxious: "She doesn't want the kids to hear that kind of talk. They admire this minister, and he's always worrying out loud over someone, or some problem." Joe dislikes all those sermons; they make him feel uncomfortable, accused, a criminal of sorts. The minister can talk as he wishes, and if need be, move on to another church; whereas people like Joe and Doris have to stay — or so Joe feels. And anyway, ministers have a way of making things much too simple and stark and apocalyptic: "To hear him talk on Sunday, you'd think we were on the verge of ruin, America, unless we solve every problem we have and especially the race problem. He's got the Negro people on his brain, our minister. He must dream about them every night. He says we're to blame, the white people, for all that's happened. I went up once after the sermon and asked him what I've done that's to blame. He said he didn't mean any one person, just the whole white world. I didn't know how I could answer him. I said I'd never wanted to hurt a Negro, all I wanted was for them to leave me alone and I'd leave them alone. But that got him going again, and I pretended that I had to leave, because we had to be somewhere. On the way home I told Doris I'm ready to start shopping for a new church, but she and the children like him, the minister. They say he's 'dynamic.' He either makes me mad or puts me to sleep. So you see, we don't agree on *everything* in this house."

Joe is at times envious. His sister is married to a schoolteacher who is a Catholic. In the Catholic Church, he believes, one is spared those sermons. In the Catholic Church one goes for mass, for communion, not to be lectured at over and over again. But his sister and brother-in-law disagree. They have also had to sit through sermons, and they have their misgivings about the direction the church is taking. Here is what his sister says: "It's not any one church, it's them all. I listen to my neighbors talk. A lot of church people are always scolding the ordinary man. If you ask me, the rich people and the college professors have too much influence with the cardinal. Even the Catholic Church can be pushed around. All of a sudden, these last few years, we've been hearing these letters from him, the cardinal. He tells us this is wrong and that is wrong, and it seems all he has on his mind is the colored people. I'm sick and tired of them and their complaining. And they've stirred up everyone; my husband tells me the children in junior high school are 'organizing.' That's what they call it. They have 'grievances,' and they want to talk about them with the teachers and the principal. I'd give them the back of my hand. I'd read them the riot act. But no, the principal is afraid that if they get 'too strict,' the teachers, then the kids will get even more aroused, and there will be more trouble. Can you imagine that? And he's talking with them — hour after hour, I hear.

"There's something wrong, that's what I say; and it all started with this civil rights business, the demonstrations, and then the college radicals and on and on. It used to be that you could go to church and pray for your family and country. Now they're worried about colored people and you even get the feeling they care more about the enemy, the people killing our boys in Vietnam, than our own soldiers. And the schools, the radicals and the colored are both trying to destroy the schools — I mean, take them over, that's what. They don't like what's being taught, and they don't like the teachers, and a day doesn't go by that they don't have something bad to say, or a new threat for us to hear. My husband says he'd quit tomorrow if he didn't have so much seniority, and if he could get another job. It's pretty bad for you these days if you're just a law-abiding, loyal American and you believe in your country, and in people being happy with their own kind, and doing their best to keep us the first in the world. And, God

11

forbid, if you say we need to keep the streets safe, and stop those riots and marches, then the priest will pull you aside and tell you that you don't 'understand.' But I do, that's the point. I understand what's happening. We're losing our freedom. We can't be ourselves anymore. There are those that want to change the country completely. They are dictators. A lot of priests are with us; but some have been fooled, and two of them are in our parish, I'll tell you."

There are differences, of course, in the two families. A teacher is not a steam fitter. Once the teacher felt himself "higher," a man of education, a man who wears a suit to work. Now the teacher feels hard pressed and bitter. His salary has for a decade been inadequate, and for half a decade he has had to work in the evenings and on weekends, even as his brother-in-law does. The high school children seem harder to control. The educational critics are constantly saying bad things about people like him, or so he feels. And everyone's sympathy seems to go elsewhere: "The priests, a lot of them feel sorry for the Negroes and the North Vietnamese. The college students love Asians and Africans, love to go work in the ghetto. Their professors keep on saying how bad our schools are. College professors make three and four times what we do, and they have the nerve to say we're not 'motivated' enough, and we don't teach the way we should. They can cry with sympathy for some insolent, fresh-talking Negro demonstrator, who wants the world delivered into his hands within twenty-four hours, but if we even try to explain our problems, they start telling us how wrong we are, and how we need to learn how to be 'open' with the children, and 'accepting,' and how we are 'rigid' and 'prejudiced,' and everything bad. I've heard them on television.

"No one asks people like me to be on television. I'm a teacher, but no educational television people come and ask me my opinion. They get these writers and 'experts' and let them say one bad thing after the other, and we're supposed to say: that's right, that's absolutely right. Not one of them impresses me as anything but a sensationalist. They love tearing things down. And you know who eats it all up, don't you: the intellectuals, the rich people out in the suburbs, the people who send their children to private schools, and then say it's awful, how we're treating the Negroes, and not keeping up with all those 'progressive' ideas, which (mind you) change every other year."

One can, of course, go on and on with tape-recorded conversations such as these, toned down here, edited there, abbreviated necessarily. One can call upon a bank teller or a barber or a repairman for the telephone company or a truck driver or a man who works in a large factory or a man who works in a small warehouse. One can call upon the electricians and carpenters who work with Joe, or other teachers who work with his brother-in-law in a high school. And then, there are clerks, accountants, salesmen, bus drivers, firemen, and policemen. If an observer wants to lump them all together, millions and millions of men, women and children, he can resort to labels and phrases, some of them more traditional than others. For a long time there have been "blue-collar workers" and "white-collar workers"; and there has been the "lower middle class." More than any other expression, though, the people themselves (as we have mentioned) like to use "ordinary man" or "average American" or "plain person." Again and again one hears those words, all the time spoken with pride and conviction and a touch of sadness, a touch of worry — as if the country has not learned to appreciate such people, and maybe even makes them pay for the sins of others, pay with their lives, their savings, their energies. And they have indeed paid. They have seen their savings mean less, or disappear, as inflation gets worse and worse. They have had to take second jobs to keep up with prices. They have sent their sons abroad, and thousands of them have died — all of which an observer knows and reads and repeats to himself from time to time and then is likely to forget.

Is it, then, a certain vulnerability that they share, those "ordinary people"? Are they best thought of as socially insecure, economically marginal, politically unorganized, hence weak? Ought we be talking about millions and millions of people in such a way; that is, do they all lend themselves to the generalizations that social scientists, journalists and politicians persist in using? Needless to say, statistics and indices of one kind or another certainly do tell a lot; they quite precisely tell us how much money comes into homes, how much is spent and by whom — that is, people employed where and of what educational "level" or background. But again, one must ask whether expressions like "social class" quite explain what it is that so many Americans have in common when they call themselves "ordinary." Money is part of the answer; they have some, enough to get by, *just* get by, *barely* get by, *fairly* comfortably get by. (Qualifications like "just" or "barely" or "fairly" are always there and say a good deal.) But there are other things that matter to people. How much schooling did I get? How much do I wish I'd had? How much do I want for my children? What kind of work do I do, apart from the money I make, and what kind would I like to do? Where do I live? Where would I prefer to live, if I could have my choice? Which church do I attend? How do I like to dress? And finally, do I feel at ease about my life and my future, even though I live in a good, strong house, well supplied with gadgets and appliances on the inside and surrounded by a nicely tended lawn on the outside?

II

Maybe we rarely put questions like those to ourselves so directly. But they are there, waiting to be asked, and often enough they make their presence felt. Here is a so-called blue-collar worker, a machinist speaking: "I'm happy with my life, mostly. Things could be worse. They could be better, but that's life. You never have all you want. If you did, you'd be bored. Right? I'll admit that I have my complaints. Sometimes I think I'd like to start protesting myself. But I was brought up to work and obey the law, and I'm glad I was. My dad wanted me to go to college, but I never had the mind for books. I've always been good with my hands. I like the work I do. I'll admit there will be some days I'll regret I'm not a lawyer, or some big shot. But usually I don't have time to think like that.

"I'm glad I live right here. I hate cities. I like a small town. Even though it means I have to drive a half an hour longer, I'd rather be here than near the plant. It may sound old-fashioned to you, but to me cities are where city slickers live, businessmen and lawyers and that type, and the colored people. Who wants any part of them? Not me, I'll tell you that. I've never been to New York in my life. I've never been to Chicago. There was a time that I thought I'd take my children to Washington to see the White House, you know, and the monuments; but from what I read, you're a fool to go there. You spend all that time and money getting to the place, and you get held up and maybe beaten up. It's a colored city — our capital!

"Hell, I've nothing against them, Negro people. They should stick to their own, like we do. I'm Polish. I mean, I'm American. My family has been here for four generations; that's a lot. My great-grandfather came over here, from near Cracow. I've never been to Poland. I'll never go there. Why should I? It's in your blood. It's in your background. But I live *here*. My wife is the same, Polish. We're just like other people in this country, but we have memories, Polish memories, that's what my grand-father used to say: 'John, don't let your kids forget that once upon a time the family was in Poland.' How *could* I forget? My wife won't let me. She says you have to stay with your own people. We don't have only Polish people living near us, but there are a lot. Mostly we see my family and my wife's family on the weekends, so there's no time to spend doing anything else."

True, his remarks have been extracted from a much longer conversa-

43

tion; but the themes keep coming up week after week, in talk after talk. Yes, he makes over ten thousand but less than fifteen thousand dollars a year; but just as important, he makes that money at a particular job, and he went so far but no further in school, and he wants so much though no more for himself — and for his children, too. Moreover, he lives as far away from the city as he reasonably can, and he has a certain background, which he proudly calls his own, even as he wonders, in an off-guard moment, precisely what he and the rest of us are to be called: "I don't know who's *really* an American. There are guys I work with, they're Italian and Irish. They're different from me, even though we're all Catholics. You see what I mean? We're buddies on the job. We do the same work. We drink our coffee together and sit there eating lunch. But you leave and you go home and you're back with your own people. I don't just mean my family, no. It's more than your wife and kids; it's everything in your life."

So, he resists our effort to fit him neatly into a category. He is like his co-workers, but he is also different. He is *himself*. Yet, surely there are things that bind us together, and most particularly determine how we respond to the news, the world's events. John is willing to go along with that, willing to say yes to an observer's desire that he join company with millions and stand for something, affirm certain principles that he shares with more than a given family: "If I had to sign on the dotted line, I'd say I'm an American workingman and a family man, and I like where we live and the people nearby, and I wouldn't exchange what I've got for anything else in the world, no sir! I believe that if you went and talked to people in every country of the world, they'd all wish they could be Americans. It's not only the wealth here in this country, it's the freedom. No one comes knocking on my door telling me what to believe. Once I come home and close that door, I know I'm my own boss. Even at work, there's just so far the company can push you. We'll be talking sometimes during the coffee break and we bellyache and we bellyache, but every once in a while we stop and remind ourselves that we're in America, and we have jobs, and we have our homes and our families, and we're not hungry and if it gets cold, there's heat, and now we even have an air conditioner in our bedroom. I'm not completely satisfied, but I'm not dumb. I read the papers and I see on TV what's going on in other countries.

"We're not big thinkers, none of us are. Who wants to be? I want my boy to go to college, but I'd hate to see him get a big head, full of a lot of crazy ideas, the way a lot of them do, the rich college students. There are thousands and thousands of good college students from good homes, and they never make a lot of noise and look queer — and no one puts them on television and no one writes them up in the papers. All they want is to get ahead, like anyone does. They're not the snob-students from the snob-colleges. And you know, it's not just the snob-students, anyway, that cause the trouble. It's the professors. It's the big-brain types who look down on the rest of us. I'm not ashamed of the way I think; but they'd like us to be. I mean, they'd like it if the workingman was always going to them, and asking them what he should do and who he should vote for. The way I see it, you've got these people who run the big companies; and then you've got others who run the newspapers and the magazines and the television stations, and they're all full of themselves — I'll say it, because I really believe they are. I turn on that television station we've got, and it's better than a comedy show. The way they speak on those talk shows! The announcer, with his phony English accent! And the things they say, it makes you want to go and smash the damn set! They're full of long lectures, and they're always 'reconsidering' something. They don't really like this country, that's one of the problems. There are times when I completely agree with what they'll say, but it's their *attitude* that gets you. They're conceited, that's what I'd call them. They make you want to go kick them you know where and tell them to come off it, cut it out. Like my wife says: 'Jesus Christ, it can't be that complicated!'

"They can take anything and make it into what they want. I guess they're just smart talkers. My daughter is in her first year of high school. She says that's what they are, smart talkers. You know who their pet is? It's the Negro. If I was a colored man, a Negro, I'd tell the college people to get off my back and leave me alone. There are people in this world who never forget that they went to college; that's the trouble with them. They talk as if they're trying to prove to the rest of us that they're educated and we're not. And now they've got the Negro, like a little pet dog. They're for him. Anything he does, even if he robs and kills, it's all right, because America has been bad, and hasn't treated the colored people right. I'd like to know what a lot of colored people think about those professors. I bet no more than we do."

One presses him, asks him who belongs to "we." And he has anticipated the curiosity, the interest, the question. He has heard politicians speak and read what various people have said and talked with his family and friends; he has thought things over and tried to be fair and honest and decent and kind: "I don't know if I have the right to speak for anyone except myself. Even my wife will disagree with me sometimes — and argue her beliefs against mine. What I don't like about the students, the loud-mouthed ones, is that they think they know so much they can speak for everyone, because they're right and the rest of us aren't clever enough and can't talk like they can. That's why I'm not going to be like them, and speak for everyone I work with at the plant and our whole neighborhood. But we think alike, all of us do, when you come right down to it. We'd like everyone in the country to have a fair chance. I mean, I don't want anyone lording it over me, and I don't want to lord it over anyone. If you ask me, most of us in this country think alike.

"The ones who don't think like we do I can list for you: the militants, the colored ones and the white ones, and the big business people, and the snobs, the college crowd. I don't mean the average college student who comes from an average family and is trying to better himself. I don't mean the ordinary colored man, just trying to get by, like you and me and the next guy. And the small businessman, he's in the same boat as everyone. But there are people in this country who make all the noise and have their hands on most of the money; that's what I'd say. You can split the whole of America that way; I believe you can. There's most people, regardless of whether they're Polish or Italian or Irish or anything else, including colored or Indians, and there are the people who get in the newspaper headlines and run things, or try to run things. The way I see it, the bankers still control the country. You don't see them losing out, whether we're in a depression or an inflation. And the demonstrators, they *want* to run the country. I have a friend, he and I work together, and he says he wishes they'd get rid of each other, the rich guys and the college radicals. But I guess someone has to run the banks and the stock market. If not, we'd have no country left. And you need the colleges, or else we'd slip back to poverty, the country would. I just wish the big banks and the companies would think of everyone's welfare, and not just their own; and I can't believe a kid has to become a crazy hippie and a radical, just because he's getting an education for himself."

He expands in that direction. He talks about the decent and honorable industrialists that must be around. He has never seen them; but then, he has never seen *any* industrialist in the flesh. He talks about the fine young people this country has, *including* college students, he emphasizes. He insists he understands that "there have to be all kinds." America stands for that, its historical willingness to receive hard-pressed people, offer them sanctuary, and after a brief time grant them the political rights that go with citizenship. He doesn't want any of that changed; America would no longer be America. But even so, but even so; he keeps on adding those three words. He keeps on zigzagging. He keeps on struggling with the mixed feelings he has — and he needs no visitor to point out that such is the case, that he has shifts of opinions, that he contradicts himself, goes here and there (and sometimes it seems) everywhere as he talks. In fact he is quite concerned with *position*, with where he stands and where others do; and so he uses rather often what I suppose could be called topographical or geographical imagery. He is "all over the place" in what he has said; and he can recognize that fact. He is "all over the map." He is "in the middle." He is "in the center," and "between the extremes." Indeed, he is always going up and down, crossing himself back and forth, as he talks: "I'm taking you and me for a ride, I guess. My kids tell me sometimes that I'm crossing the road when I talk with them, going back on what I just said. But I tell them you can't make life letter-perfect, because it isn't. I'd be more consistent, like they want, if the world would let me be."

What about the world? Is he hopeful, in general? Is he as gloomy most of the time as he sometimes can be? What bothers him most? What pleases him most? I suspect that he couldn't (why should he?) take a battery of questions like that without laughing, without feeling sorry for the poor soul who can't just live and let things be — and *do* rather than *ask*. Still, John can understand how people would want to know what other people are thinking. He has never been questioned by a "pollster," but if he were to be, he would do his best to come up with answers that are clear-cut, unambiguous, worth the interrogator's time and effort. As a matter of fact, he reads "those polls." He is not sure he trusts them, though. He is not sure he believes them. Who is sought out, after all, and asked to come up with all those opinions? No one John has ever known. Sometimes he even wonders whether the blind don't lead the blind: "People read in the papers that other people think this thing or the next. Then they get asked, and then they say what they think the majority thinks. I believe that it's very hard to stick with your own beliefs. To be honest, we'll all be sitting there in the cafeteria eating our sandwiches, and one guy will say something, and then you can see everyone wondering what they think. The ones who talk loudest and are strong, you know — their personality is strong — they are the ones you go along with. I mean, if you disagree with them, you keep quiet. If you agree, you nod and say 'that's right.' I'll be sitting there some of the time, and I'll wonder what those buddies of mine *really* believe.

"Of course, I don't know what *I* think about a lot of subjects. I'm glad I have those machines to work on. I honestly don't know how people can spend all their time talking, talking, the way politicians do. I tell my kids, I hope they go as far as they can, education-wise, but they should never get dizzy on the stuff, all those words and degrees." He laughs when he says that. He doesn't really think he has to explain himself, though. Going to college can be like drinking. Take a lot of beer, take a few shots of whiskey, and you get high. You lose your judgment. You overestimate yourself and you forget about the most obvious and important things. Likewise, one can read and read and read, and get lost in a world of theories, an unreal world. He lists the dangers, recites one of them after another, each begining with "you." Then he catches himself, and observes that maybe he is being unfair. He is speaking about himself, not necessarily anyone else, certainly not everyone else. *He* would get lost and confused if he read too many books. That's the point. And that's the trouble in this world, the big trouble: people constantly speak for other people.

There is, for instance, a Negro in the plant. He's been there about a year. At first he seemed slow, inadequate, poorly coordinated, just the kind of person the "civil rights people" are pushing on factories and schools and neighborhoods and God knows what and whom next. ("They'll be wanting us to entertain them in our houses before long!") But even so, John tried to be nice to the guy. He doesn't have it in him to kick a guy, especially when he's down. He explains why: "The colored are a persecuted people. I know that. I've said to my wife a few times that I wouldn't mind being born Irish or German, even Italian. I'd sooner be Chinese than a Negro. That's how you can tell how you feel, by what you'd be willing to be, if you had to be turned into something else. That's why I tried to help the guy. I've talked with them, each of them they've hired to work with us. I notice it takes a few of us to break the ice for them. They're afraid of us, I guess. But they don't talk the way we do, and you've got to go slow. I'd be like that myself if I was one of them.

"But after a while you see they're all different, like we are. The man I was starting to tell you about, he's no buddy of mine, but he *could* be. He's just another man on the job there, in the plant. I don't even think of him as colored, or like that. I forget. We all do. I'll hear a guy remind himself sometimes. He'll say, 'He's colored.' No one would want to call that man a 'nigger.' He's not one. There's a difference. I'm not ashamed to call some of them 'niggers.' They are. Two little nigger kids knocked my sister-in-law down. They stole her pocketbook, right in broad daylight, downtown. She reported it to the police. They told her the little bastards come into town, looking for women walking alone, and rush them, and they're gone before you know it. The newspapers don't have their long editorials about that. You know what the police told her, my sister-in-law? They said she shouldn't come shopping in the city, white people shouldn't. They should stay where they live and shop in the shopping centers near their homes. The niggers wouldn't dare go there. 'Let them have the downtown city,' that's what one of the policemen, the sergeant, said. But my sister-in-law answered him back. She said she likes those big stores, and she's not living in some rich suburb where the best stores have branches. So, what are we supposed to do when we want to do Christmas shopping? The sergeant said we'd better 'reverse our direction' and drive outward and not in to town. My sister-in-law said she used the subway — she hasn't got a car. Her husband takes the car to work. The sergeant said, 'Lady, I know, I know. It's too complicated for me.' That's the way I feel. I think a lot of people do; they feel all mixed up about what's going on in this country today."

Again and again he mentions how "mixed-up" he feels about various social and political issues. He is "in the middle so far as that goes." He is of two minds about something; and he doesn't know where he stands on something else — though, again, he *is* aware of and *does* appreciate his own inconsistencies. Outside observers, always trying to spot trends, comprehend patterns, and figure out exactly (nothing less!) what is going on, can easily do him an injustice by assuming that he, unlike those who make studies and do research, doesn't see a contradiction when it emerges in the course of a conversation. But the fact is that right after the words quoted immediately above were spoken, some other remarks of substantial interest followed: "I don't think anyone really knows what's going on while he's in the middle of it. I tell my children that America is changing. I guess you have to have changes. You can't stay still. The colored people need more changes than anyone, though I hear the Indians have it real bad, too. It's always tough for poor people when they're trying to get their share of the pie. No one wants to give up what he has. The bosses fought the labor unions. The old-time people here in America never wanted Irish and Italians to live near them. I never thought about it like that, but one of my kids came home and told us that the teacher said something about the colored people having to fight their way into America, like other people have, and I thought at first it was the usual propaganda, but the more I heard the kid talk, the more I thought maybe he was right.

"Of course, I think people have been spoiling the colored people; I mean the rich college kids who get their big thrills by going into a slum and telling all those niggers how nice and wonderful they are. If I was a nigger I'd tell those rich white people from the big, fat suburbs and the colleges to get the hell out and leave me alone. But if a man is in trouble, I can feel sorry for him, and I think the colored man is in trouble; he's not getting a fair shake from the country. I believe that's true. Don't ask me what should be done, though. I don't know. One minute I'll say we ought to give them a break, the colored, and the next minute I'll be fed up with them, like when they're marching all over the place, demonstrating, or rioting, or when their kids go stealing pocketbooks and pulling knives on people and all that. Who can agree with himself all the time? Not me! We'll be talking at the plant, and we catch each other contradicting what we just said, and we laugh. It's crazy, the world; that's what I believe. You can't make sense of people. They're too mixed-up."

People like him possess a richness and complexity of thinking that often enough social observers (writers or university-based scholars) simply fail to notice. People like him can be as unfairly caricatured or labeled as black people are by open, unashamed bigots. People like him in moments of honesty and passion can cry out for sympathy and understanding. People like him notice others getting attention, concern, gestures of friendship; so they feel twinges of envy — though they also want no condescending nod from snobbish outsiders, commentators, observers. People like him are fighters, are stubborn, are hard workers, feel great pride in what they do, know love as well as hate, laugh at things as well as fear things, reach out to people as well as run and hide from them, cursing and enraged.

49

III

HERE FOR EXAMPLE is a policeman talking, not the sergeant just mentioned above, but another sergeant, one also convinced that things are "too complicated" for him, but not about to say so, not directly at least, even if the conversation with the visitor is the thirty-fourth one, and the first one was well over a year before: "Why does everyone say the police are against the Negroes? I'm sick of hearing that. *The police!* There are thousands and thousands of policemen, and they're individuals, just like everyone else. The same people who say they want us to recognize that Negroes are like other people — good and bad and not-so-good and not-so-bad — are the ones who call us every name in the book. We're bigots. We're pigs. We're killers. We're flunkies. We're storm troopers. We're ignorant and fascists — and on and on they go. Have you ever seen those college kids shouting at the police? I've never seen anything like them for meanness and cheapness. The language that comes out of their mouths; you begin to wonder whether you're in a mental hospital. I mean it; those kids go crazy when they see us. The uniform seems to trigger something in them. They become dirty, plain dirty. They use the worst language I've ever heard. They make insulting gestures at us. They talk about killing us. The girls make sexual overtures — when they're not swearing. Swearing, that's not the word for what you hear! Someone has never really taught those wise-guy kids good manners. They say they're out to help the poor; but I'll take a Negro kid to them any day. The Negroes have a lot to teach those college radicals.

"I laugh at times, though; I laugh at the radicals and I laugh at the Negro people. They think they're living under a dictatorship, and that the police are out to get them. The fact is that the poor policeman, he has to watch himself all the time. He can't do half the things the radicals claim he does; and he can't say what they say he says. The policeman's hands are tied. And so is his salary; he gets paid not much more than people on welfare. He's in constant danger. We lose men; they're shot, knifed, beaten up. It seems I'm always visiting a buddy in the hospital. And we don't get flowers from radicals, saying they sympathize with us, because 'if a man dies, the world is smaller.' You know where I heard that? From them, the students. They were protesting something, a Panther's death, which they said we caused, which we didn't, and we had to arrest them — after warning them a hundred times and listening to them dare us and tease us and swear at us and push themselves at us for three hours. In jail I tried to help them out. I had to get their signatures on some forms. They refused. All we wanted to do was keep their watches from getting lost. They kept on shouting: 'If a man dies, the world is smaller.' I got angry, but I tried to joke. I said maybe the world would be smaller in a day or two, if they didn't shut up and let us do our work. They'd been calling us murderers all afternoon, but now they said I was a Nazi, the kind of man Hitler was. I thought they were fooling. I honestly did, at first. I'd even said 'please' to them, on the street and in jail. I *asked* them to be quiet and orderly. I *asked* them to move back. I *asked* them to clear away for the sake of pedestrians and cars. The nicer you are to them, the worse they get. God, they're a filthy-mouthed bunch of little bastards.

"I went to confession later and told the priest that I'd sworn back at them, I'd cursed them, and I was sorry, I really was. Did I hit them, strike at them, he asked me. I said no. Were they 'provoking' me, he asked me. I said yes, yes, Father, so help me God, they were. He said I shouldn't feel bad. He said that Christ had been afraid and worried while He was on the Cross; and if that was the case, we're all entitled to lose our tempers every once in a while. Then he said he wanted me to know, apart from his being a priest, that he was behind us in what we're trying to do, the police. I figured that if he was getting friendly, I'd be friendly, too. I said: 'Father, if you know what we're trying to do, I wish you'd let me know, and that would be two of us that knew.' I didn't hear a sound out of him. Then he asked me if I had anything more to tell him. I figured he thought I was being fresh, but I wasn't being like that. What *are* we doing, the police? We're like those students; we want to know whose fat we're pulling out of the fire. No one comes and talks to us, and asks us *our* opinions, not like they do with the college students and the Negro people. A day doesn't go by that I don't see a poll that says the students want this, or something else, and the Negroes, too — they want, want, that's all they're capable of, wanting. Well, we want some things, too. We want better salaries. We want more men on the force. We want the public to understand what we have to do, every day, to keep the city from becoming a jungle. It's not exaggerated, what you see on television. Between smart gangsters, all kinds of them, and dumb hoodlums, and the Negroes, and the drunks, and the college crowd and their demonstrations, and the crazy ones walking the street when they should be locked up — between all those, it's a miracle more of us don't get killed on the police force.

"I said to a television man once, after he took pictures of the college kids sitting all over the sidewalk near a high school, that he should let us speak to the American public. All people see is us arresting someone, or trying to clear away a mob. They don't know what we have to listen to and put up with. But if you can't take it, I suppose you shouldn't be a cop.

5¹

I tell my men that. They laugh at me and tell me to stop. I mean it though; I'm not fooling. Sure, I lose my control. Sometimes I wish I could go and kill some of those demonstrators. And as for the Negroes, I wish the average American worker could see what we see: the stealing that goes on, and the knives they have, and the razor blades they pull on each other, and the way they all loaf and collect welfare, and the way the men move from woman to woman, and leave each one of them with kids. They don't care, they don't care how they live and what they do to the buildings! A lot of people feel sorry for the 'slum landlords,' that's what they call them. How many people have seen what those kids do to the buildings? And their parents don't give a damn. They just laugh. And let me tell you; sometimes that's all *I* can do, laugh — and talk to myself. I do a lot of that. I even carry on a conversation with myself! I say that a cop can only do the best he can, and he has to be honest and fair, as honest and fair as he can be, and the worst thing he can do is forget that. People say we're crooks, we're bribed left and right. People say we're working for the big corporations and the politicians. People say we're unsympathetic to the poor. Some cops *are* like that. But a lot aren't.

"I'll tell you who the police are. They're men from plain, ordinary families. They don't have rich, fast-talking parents. They don't have parents who make all kinds of money by climbing over other people until they get on top, then start feeling sorry for the poor Negro, or the poor Puerto Rican, or whoever it is. They're not full of a lot of big talk about how they want to change the world, and help everyone out, and bring us freedom and peace and all the rest. But I'll tell you something, they're good men, a lot of policemen; they work long hours, and they don't get rich, even if they do pick up a few extra dollars now and then, some of them. They go to church. They try to bring up their kids to respect older people and obey the law. They send their sons into the army, so the country will be the strongest on the earth, and they teach their daughters to be good wives and good mothers.

"You're going to say I'm building up the policeman, and I'm not mentioning that there are plenty of bad things they do. Look, in any organization you'll find no-good people. There are rotten apples right in my own backyard; our precinct has some crazy cops who are ready to use machine guns against the 'college kids and niggers,' that's how they are called. But for every cop like that I can find you two that you'd just have to admire. I really mean it, *admire*. Every day at work they save people's lives, and protect people, and help people. They help people cross the streets. They help people when they need a ride to the hospital. They help them when they're scared of something. They help them when they've been robbed or assaulted or there's been a fire or they need to know how to get someplace and can't find their way. I've listened to those students talk about 'helping mankind,' and how much they 'love' people and how much they believe in 'giving' themselves to other people. I wonder how much they actually practice what they preach. They talk a lot, I know that. They march up and down advertising to the world how right they are and wrong everyone else is, and how much love they feel for humanity and how bad the cops are and most of the world, it seems. But do they ever really go and prove their good intentions?

"You'll say I'm prejudiced, but I honestly believe a lot of those long-haired radical students are spoiled brats from rich families who won't lift a finger for anyone who's not part of their own group. It's talk, talk, talk with them and dirty filthy talk, to be exact. The same goes for the civil rights people, a lot of them. They're for the Negro they say; but the police are helping Negroes every hour, day and night. You look surprised. You see, that's the trouble! People just don't know. They don't stop and think. They forget that it's the cops who come and take sick Negroes to the hospital, and rescue them from killing each other. Have you ever seen the way those drugged-up niggers go after each other with knives and blades. It's unbelievable. I'm not prejudiced when I say that colored people have a lot of violence in them, like animals. The Irishman will get sloppy drunk and pass out. The Italian will shout and scream his head off. The Jew will go figure out a way he can make himself a little more money, and get even with someone that way. But your nigger, he's vicious like a wild leopard or something when he's been drinking or on drugs. They throw lye at each other, and scalding water, and God knows what. I tell my men to stay away, stay away. It's a jungle. They drove the Jews out, and they're not store-keepers themselves; they don't know how to run a store. And now it's a ghost town, the colored section.

"The Negroes want more kids, to get more welfare money, and they want to push into new districts. You can get fed up with them; but you can feel sorry for them, too. They didn't ask to come here, did they? They were slaves, you can't forget that. And they treated them like animals, down there in the South, from what you read. They never let them even vote, or make a half-decent living. And they kept them separate, under the law. No Irishman or Italian or Jew ever had to live like that here in America! The average cop knows that, too. It's just that he's all the time seeing the results, not the causes of things. I wish the big, smart college people would get that through their heads, that someone has to be there on the firing line, protecting the whole of American society from what it's done wrong in the past. I believe that slowly things will get better, for the Negro I mean. I *don't* believe we'll see an improvement in the way the rich college kids behave, though. *There's* where I see our main trouble coming from in the next ten years. The Negroes, a lot of them, will begin to feel more part of America; but those kids, they're another story. They hate this country. They're full of hate, the radical kids. The Negroes only want

53

more of America. Some of the radicals want to blow the whole country up. They're lunatics, I believe.

"You're the doctor. Maybe you know what's bothering them. I listen to them; I should know. But I don't. I can't believe it's what they *say* it is, that they're just upset about injustice. There's something that's under their skin. They have a grudge against the world. They never smile, you know. They're mean. I've tried to get on with them, make a joke or two; but no, they hiss and spit and make faces and come out with the worst language I've ever heard in my life. Listen, I'm a cop, from poor people; and they had no education to speak of, my mother or my dad, and he was a long-shoreman. But let me tell you, I get red in the face, I blush, when I hear those kids talk. And, it's not from being mad at them, either. I've just never heard such words come out, one after the other, and nonstop, all day and all night, so long as you stand and listen. It's those kids, and the older ones they depend upon — the lawyers, the teachers on their side — that we're going to have around with us for a long time. I don't get discouraged too much about our Negro people. They'll lift themselves up, a lot of them will, in time. But these rich, spoiled, college kids, drugged up on all kinds of stuff, and with their parents waiting, ready to bail them out and give them money to loaf on, we'll have more and more of those kids around. The worst thing about them is that they've never really worked for more than a few weeks, here and there. And when they call a 'strike' on a campus, they're supposed to get clemency and be excused from exams and every-thing else. Do they know what a *real* strike is? Do they know the sacrifices that strikers make and *expect* to make and don't always brag about? I hear those college people talking about how they're different, they're not like everyone else, and they can't respect what the rest of us do. No wonder; they've never had to get up in the morning and go to work, and stay on the job, whether they like it or not, and pay their bills or try to pay them. Does anyone except the rich keep up with his bills, these days?"

Things run into one another eventually; and so the students eventually give way to inflation in a policeman's mind. He is a tall, rather heavy man, full of stories, and they are stories he has earned, stories he has lived through. He loves "the beat." He loves walking down a street, driving down a street, catching the sense of a neighborhood, feeling its rhythms. They are all different, those various neighborhoods, he lets his listener know, and goes on to tell why and how in direct language. He doesn't miss much while patroling a street. His mind can be subtle, canny, practical and yes, open to change. That is, he can be dogmatic and bitter one minute, then come around to a longer, more reflective viewpoint. It is then that he summons history, recalls past events, speculates about the future. It is then that he sums up what he has gone through, what others have also gone through, what a whole world has had to experience.

To some extent he feels a little shy about revealing his considerable

54

powers of observation and reflection. He doesn't want to be caught spinning a lot of fancy theories. He doesn't want to be like those wordy, brainy protesters and demonstrators and radicals. He doesn't want to sound like an "expert" on the one hand or an "agitator" on the other. He is tired of experts; they call themselves criminologists and sociologists and psychologists and they want to lecture to the police and tell them in fancy language what "any cop" knows out of his everyday, concrete experience. They go on and on, delivering those "lectures" he and his friends are ordered by "the Chief" to hear, and the men, most of them, get annoyed and angry. It is not that they feel they have nothing to learn; it is simply that "professors aren't practical, and they can't talk straight." Nevertheless, there is a lot of worry about, a lot happening, and a lot of help is needed by policemen as well as other people. And there is the irony; sympathy and compassion are mobilized for blacks and Indians and Mexican-Americans by all sorts of thoughtful and well-educated people, but the police and their serious difficulties are often ignored by those same people. Why is it that some of us do that, overlook or try hard to "understand" the meanness and brutishness and open violence to be found among the poor (among other groups of people) but jump upon the police with a whole range of epithets, some of them openly nasty, some thinly disguised with a veneer of academic jargon? He asks that question again and again, in many different ways. Sometimes he can be self-pitying when he asks. Sometimes he can be angry. Often he is genuinely puzzled. When the question is put back to him he pleads ignorance, or he becomes silent, or he talks and talks and talks. Yes, he acknowledges, some policemen are unthinking and crooked and even cruel. Yes, some are bigots, pure and simple. Yes, the police upon occasion lose their cool, wrongly go after people and at the same time shelter others considered friendly or "patriotic." But in any occupation, any profession, any group of human beings one will find a wide range of people, and he feels that the "so-called liberals" don't mobilize their considerable powers of compassion or understanding for everyone, "just for certain people."

Over and over again he makes that point. He would like, one day, to talk with some of "them," the people who call the police so many bad names, who look upon them as the enemy, who say the ghettoes ought to be "freed of the pigs." On the other hand, he is afraid that were the occasion to arise he would be so enraged and provoked by the way "those people" look and talk, by their attitude toward him and his kind, that he would have to leave immediately; or if he did stay, he worries that he would be unable to state his case. Yet, he does want to talk about some of these matters, and by no means is he as sure of himself as others say he is, or as he himself sometimes says he is.

The sergeant more than anything else regrets the breakdown of old customs and habits. In addition he cannot understand what will replace those customs and habits, especially because things seem so unstable, so uncertain, so unpredictable. He senses all kinds of shifts in public opinion. He listens to people all day, and has come to realize how troubled and fearful they are, how buffeted by rising prices and the demands of our armed services for men and more men. Many people read of such things, pride themselves on knowing what is happening in America, yet cannot comprehend (so he believes, so many policemen believe) the particular stresses that fall on those who are "caught in the middle." If he prefers any expression it is that one. He and others are destined to be caught in the middle, and he adds to those words three others meant to emphasize a certain finality in the predicament: "and that's it." If asked whether he sees any changes forthcoming, has any hope about the immediate future, he says "no" and repeats himself, says exactly what he has said before: "We're caught in the middle, and that's it." But he will go on talking. He will declare emphatically his faith in America, in its institutions and its history. He will go back on his own remarks and refute them, acknowledge that he has been wrong and will be wrong. And is he not human? Has he not the right to "let off steam," he asks, and take to task a lot of "noisy people, in love with their own voices"?

He can criticize even that effort at self-justification. The police *are* different. In a way they don't have the rights others do, the right to take sides and show their alarm or rage or apprehension. If a man is to be a good policeman he has to be "neutral." He has to *feel* neutral. Naturally, it is impossible to do so, deny one's convictions and allegiances. Still, one has to try; and one can within limits succeed. Nor does he have in mind "a lot of talking." Nor does he favor "these groups you hear about." (Yes, "sensitivity training groups" have been recommended for the police.) He does not want his men becoming too introspective, saying everything that's on their minds. "Hell, if we got to doing that, we'd have no time to do our work, and let me tell you, we'd be walking around like zombies, always wondering what someone else is thinking. That's no way to live."

In fact, he has been to "a couple of those things." He had been asked to take part in a "group" sponsored by a "human relations outfit, they called themselves." He went. He went because he wanted to learn something. He went because he was curious and also a little desperate. His men are under great strain, get thoroughly inadequate salaries, and at times seem on the verge of quitting en masse. He is a little older than some of them, a little younger "but wiser" than others. He wants to do what he can to "clear the air," make the men he works with "a little happier about their work." So he went, and found himself being asked one question after the other by people who smiled at him and told him they "understood" how he felt, but were, so he believed, "real strangers," by which he meant "always wanting to bury anything you say in a long afternoon of speeches."

Is he an "ordinary cop," as he once called himself? Is he a "boss," a "sergeant boss," as he refers to himself sometimes with mixed pride and embarrassment? Is he a "fascist pig," as he is called, among other things, by bright, vocal college students who are taking courses in sociology and psychology and political science and economics and urban affairs and law — and who prompt from him a wider range of responses than they might believe possible, for all their unquestionable awareness and sharpness of mind? It is, of course, possible to list those responses, and yet somehow no list, however well drawn up and accurately phrased, quite seems to render truthfully a man's ideas as they come tumbling out in the course of talk after talk — all of which is rather obvious not only to "investigators" and "observers" doing their "research" but those very able and sensitive and strong-minded and independent and mean-spirited and inefficient and awkward and generous and sullen and lighthearted and callous and kind people who are "interviewed."

More than anything else the police sergeant resents "propaganda" about the police, his way of describing "those articles about our problems." He is tired of them, tired of "dumb reporters" doing "quickie stories on the cops," and tired of "smart-aleck graduate students and their professors" who are always going to police headquarters and wanting to interview someone on the force. Can't they simply go strike up a conversation with a cop, buy him a beer, get to know him, learn "whatever in hell it is" they want to know *that way?* Can't they do anything without those folders and the questions, dozens and dozens of questions? Life for him is too complicated for a questionnaire. Life for him is hard to put into any words, "even your own, never mind someone else's." It is easy to argue with him, or applaud him because he says what seems eminently sensible and correct. It is more important, perhaps, for all of us to understand that he is not so much against one or another "method" of research as he is doubtful that "a policeman or a fireman or a man who works on an assembly line of a factory" is going to get the compassion and fair treatment he deserves from people who make it their business to be known as compassionate and fair-minded: "The worst insults the police get is from the liberals and the radicals. A suburban housewife called up the other day and demanded to speak with 'the lieutenant.' She said she belonged to some committee, I didn't catch the name. She said we were the worst people in America, and if a Hitler ever took over here, we'd be marching people into concentration camps. Now, you know, that's not the first time I've heard that. Every time we get called to a college campus we get told things like that; and not only by the kids. Their teachers can be just as bad. I'd like to give each of them a jab to the stomach and a jab to the jaw. But I can't. And I tell my men that *they* can't, either.

"Very few people know what it's like to have the radicals shouting at you from one direction and the Negro people in the slums looking at you as if you hate each and every one of them, and the people in between, most white people, claiming you've failed them, too, because there's crime all

57

over, and it's the fault of the police, *the police*. I go to work somedays and tell myself I'm going to quit. The men all say that. I don't know a policeman who feels he's being treated right. We don't get nearly the money we should, considering the fact that every hour we take risks all the time and could be killed almost every minute of the working day. And even our best friends and supporters don't know what we do — the calls that come in for our help, the duties we have. You go and ask the average Negro in a Negro neighborhood about the police, and he won't talk the way the civil rights people do. They call us all the time, Negroes do. I used to work in one of their districts. The switchboard was busy all day and all night. They fight and squabble with each other. They drink a lot. They lose themselves on drugs. They rob and steal from each other. They take after each other and kill. Then people say it's us, the police, the white man, that's to blame.

"I know I keep telling you all that, but people don't understand. I have one wish. I wish I could take some of those student radicals and send them out with some of my men that work in the Negro sections. I think it would open up their eyes, the students — that is, if anything can. They'd see that if you pulled the police out of the Negro sections, like the white radicals say you should — *they* don't live there! — then the ones who would suffer would be the poor, innocent, colored people. They're always the ones to suffer. A lot of Negroes are like a lot of white folks — good people, real good people.

"I hear my men talking. They say what I do. I have a brother who's a fireman. He says the same thing: it's not the average colored man who's to blame for all the trouble we're having in this country. It's a handful; well, it's more than a handful of troublemakers. There are the crazy agitators, and the college crowd, the students and the teachers, and worst of all, if you ask me, are the rich people who support them all, and come into the city to march and demonstrate and wave their signs. Maybe it's all for the good, though. I've given up figuring out the answers. There's a whole lot of injustice in America. I know that. I can't afford for anyone in my family to get sick, least of all myself. The rich get richer and the poor ordinary man, he can barely buy his food and pay his rent. I feel sorry for the Negroes, I really do. People are prejudiced, most people are. You're almost born that way, don't you think? People like to stick together. The Irish want to live near the Irish. The same with the Italians or the others. Jews always stick together, even when they get rich, and a lot of them do. The poor Negroes, they want to get away from each other. They want to break out. I don't blame them. But when they break out what will they find? They'll see that the Irish are no good, and the Italians and Jews and everyone. We're all no good. I believe you should know the man, not where his grandfather came from. I mean, people like their own, but that isn't the way it should be. My son comes home and tells me that his teacher says the world is always changing. Well, you know it *is* always changing. I can remember a different world, the one I grew up in. That's gone, that world. A Negro boy born today is growing up in a country really worried over his people. I think everyone accepts the fact that we've got to end poverty and give people an even break, whether their skin is black or brown or whatever color it is.

"When I was a kid of twenty-five, I used to patrol a Negro section of this city. All was quiet then, no riots and no talk of revolution, and all the rest. I knew a lot of Negro people. They were poor, but they were polite and friendly. I'd get dozens of offers of coffee or a drink. We could talk, easy, real easy, with each other. Now all I hear is how no white man is trusted over there in that section. So, I asked one of my buddies, who's a sergeant like me, and over in the district I used to be in — I asked him how he could stand it over there. He said he was surprised at me talking that way. I said I was surprised at *him* talking that way. He said it wasn't the same all the time, because they'd had a small riot or two, but it was the same as it always was most of the time: women who have to be rushed to the hospital to deliver their babies, and fires, and robberies, and fights to help settle, and kids caught on a roof or hurt playing who need to go to the emergency ward — you know, a cop's job. Then I thought to myself that I was a real fool for not thinking like that in the first place. You let those news stories go to your head, and you forget that most Negro people are too busy for demonstrations; they go to work, like the rest of us.

"I'd like to see more Negro policemen. I have nothing against them. But I don't believe in hiring a man just because he's colored or white or Chinese or anything else. If a man is going to be a policeman these days he's got to be tough. The world is tough; it's tougher than it ever was. Sometimes I look at my kids and hope they'll be all right when they grow up. I hope they'll have a world to live in."

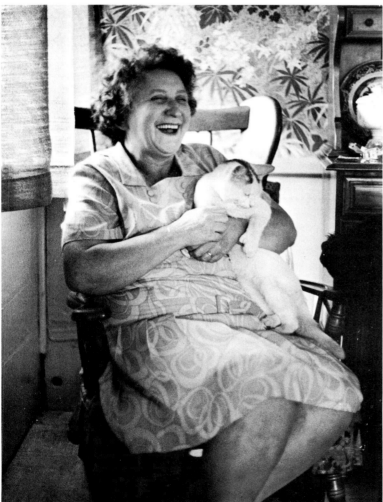

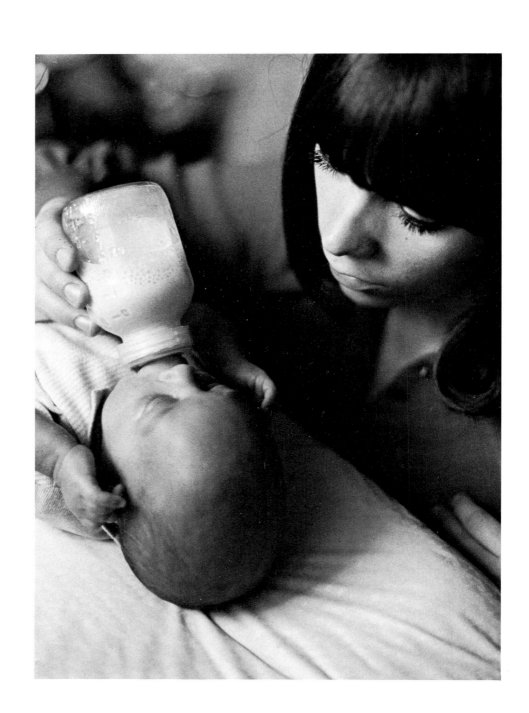

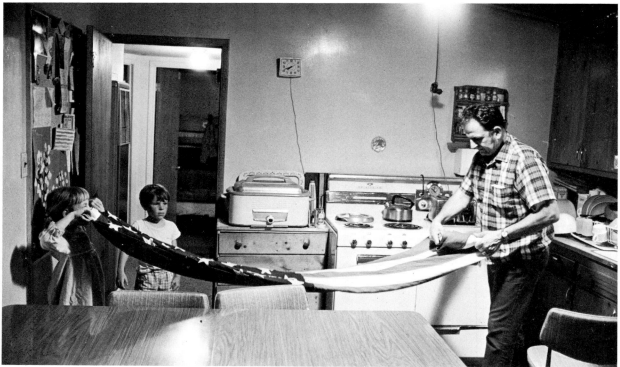

IV

THUS DOES A MAN HOPE AND WORRY and most of all work — long hours as a policeman and long hours at odd jobs, painting and carpentry. Nearby lives another man who also works long, long hours. He works for a bank. He used to be a teller, but now he helps people open accounts, advises people on which kind of loan is best, and in general is less at the mercy of the more mechanical and exhausting side of bank life. He has five suits, and changes them often. He is a neat, tidy, quiet-spoken man, not the kind inclined to answer anyone's prying questions. He quite literally is a white-collar worker: "I must have twenty white shirts. They're the only kind I *do* have. I was never allowed to wear any other color when I was a teller, and now that I'm free to dress as I please, so long as it's in good taste, I don't believe I'd like to try any new styles of clothing; and I really do like white shirts. They're the cleanest-looking, and you know where you stand with them. If they get dirty, you can see it, the dirt."

He lives in a clean house. His wife is a careful, methodical house-keeper. She loves to hear the noise of the vacuum cleaner. She uses that vacuum cleaner every day. She puts out a new shirt and pair of socks and set of underwear for her husband every night. In general she "matches the bank" in keeping things "orderly." He used that word often, "orderly." He likes his wife's "orderly nature." He is himself "orderly." What he likes about his work is the "orderly routine" he can keep: to work at a certain hour, lunch at a certain hour, home at a certain hour. When he was a child his mother took very sick. There was no one to come in and help her. They were poor. His father worked in a Western Union office, and feared he would be fired if he asked for a week or two leave of absence to take care of his children. Those were bad times, the thirties. The companies were "heartless." They could have all the workers they needed, and be as fussy, demanding and inconsiderate as they pleased. The labor unions were weak, to say the least, and the workers glad to have any job. Many of course had no work at all, and by "many" one should spell out the number, "millions and millions."

And so a man recalls his past. Born in 1934, he is "fast approaching forty." His mother eventually recovered, but not fully. She never could quite manage to take care of herself, the home, the children. In 1941 she died. Had she received better medical care she might have lived. Had there been more money around, her last years would have been more comfortable. Instead she worried; all the time she did. A maiden sister of hers, *very* clean, *very* tidy, came to take care of her at the end, and stayed to care for her two sons. But "with mother gone, something died in all of us." The father did not marry again. Western Union became his life. He has received his watch, his certificate of service, his letters of commendation. He lingers on. He has long since been replaced by "younger blood," but he is allowed to come back and watch and talk and sometimes help out. ("You'd be surprised: there are busy seasons, when a lot of people send telegrams, even with the telephone and the U.S. mail as competitors.") Meanwhile the son at the bank is glad to have his father live with him, and indeed is proud of the old man, and proud particularly of what the old man has faced in his life, lived with, struggled against, managed to overcome. "Every time I used to hear on television those spoiled-brat students singing 'we shall overcome' I'd think of my dad. *There's* someone who has overcome, let me tell you. The poor man lost his father before he ever knew him. He was killed working in a coal mine. Then his mother died, giving birth to a child, and there was no money for a doctor. My father was sent to an aunt, and she was the one who was the making of him. She didn't have the money to keep him in school, so he never got through high school; but he got a job in Western Union when he was thirteen, and he's been working for them ever since.

"My father always would preach to us. I used to think he should become a minister. Once I told him that. He said, no. He said he only wanted us to succeed, my brother and I, where he hadn't. He didn't want to preach. He wanted to help us out. He used to laugh and say that he was a graduate of the college of hard knocks, that was his college. He wanted my brother and me to go to college, but he didn't have the money; and trying to get good doctors to see my mother before she died meant that my father was paying their bills for years and years.

"I got my first job delivering papers when I was seven years old and I've been working ever since. It's a good thing I *like* to work. These days you either work or you drown. I work in the bank, then I work as a guard in a warehouse. The president of the bank owns the warehouse, and he was the one that gave a couple of us a chance to work there. I hated to take that job. I know the odds are that I'll never have to use the gun, but the fact of having it scares me. The boss said to us that it was all for show, because he didn't expect us to fight a gun battle with any robbers who come. He said most people would be scared off, just by the sight of us, and that was all he expected us to do, patrol the place and use our flashlights and be there in case of fire or to open the place sometimes for a late delivery. You know what gets to me? I feel like I'm a different person when I go there. I can't wear a suit or a shirt and tie. I put on my windbreaker jacket and a sports shirt. I'd look like a first-class fool if I showed up there dressed proper, like at the bank."

He worries about appearances — as do a lot of people, including some social critics who would quickly take note of his preoccupation with how he looks, and attribute it to his "lower middle class insecurity," but find it less easy to take a searching look at themselves and the appearances they cultivate if not worry about. He can sometimes look (and enjoy looking) impeccably groomed, whereas at other times he obviously pays little attention to what he is wearing. He can be, in his words, "a Dr. Jekyll and Mr. Hyde" about such matters, and he can in a relaxed moment take note of other variations in his life, his thinking, his mood: "My daughter is only ten years old, but she's told me a couple of times that I contradict myself. Her mother says so, too. They're right. Who doesn't contradict himself? The politicians who run this country do all the time. They're always explaining themselves. They're always trying to explain why they talk out of both sides of their mouths. When I'm in the bank I'm more likely to be tough on our customers. I'm out to do the best I can for the bank. A lot of the people I talk with are really having a bad time. Interest rates are so high, and a person who needs money for an emergency is caught in a trap; he has to pay for the money he needs. And *does* he pay! I can't let myself feel sorry for everyone I see all day long. I can't. Sometimes when I'm sitting in the warehouse and the clock is all the company I have, except my transistor radio, I'll get to thinking, and some of those poor souls I've talked with will come back to me.

"Like my father used to tell us, it's a mean, rotten world if you don't have any money. And there I am in the bank, deciding if people will get money — but I myself don't have very much! We're always behind on bills; and we run a tight ship, my wife and I — no waste and no luxuries except what we can pay for. I hate borrowing money; maybe because I see what happens to people who do. It's like quicksand; they fall into it, and they nearly die trying to get out. And the banks and finance companies are whispering in everyone's ear that they can have money (just come on in and sign a piece of paper!) and the commercials on television are telling you every half minute to buy this, and buy that, or else you'll really be behind the times and left out.

"I really think a psychiatrist could learn a lot just sitting at my desk and listening to what I hear all day. I try to do the best I can. I try to be sympathetic. But what can I do? The money isn't *mine*. I tell them that. I tell them that I only work for the bank. The things I hear people say! If they all went and did what they said they'd like to do, we'd have a revolution in this country. But people lose their tempers, and then they quiet down. They say things they regret. One old lady, she must have been eighty, told me the bankers are keeping the interest rates up to make more money. And frankly, I'll have to admit that I couldn't explain to her why interest rates *are* so high; I'm not completely sure myself. I mean, I know a lot of the reasons, but even the smartest economists have their different theories. Anyway, that old lady, she went on and on about "the few" who are ruining America, and making it tough on the rest of us. Then, you know what she told me? She's a member of the John Birch Society, and so is her son and her two daughters and their husbands! I couldn't help myself. I said, 'Lady, how will the John Birch Society change things in this country?' She said that when the conspiracy is exposed, that's ruining the country, we'd be better off. The way she sees it, the big bankers and people like that have been taken in by the Communists, and they're set upon ruining the country, and making more money while they do, and then the Russians will take over. Now, she's just crazier than the others, but you ought to hear people talk! You ought to hear how they feel. You can anticipate what they're going to say; probably it's because when they come to the bank they're all upset, and it's the moment when they really are forced to stop and think about the country and how it works and who owns things and controls things. Most of the time I don't let myself think about *that*, no sir. You get too upset — just like you do when those people you've seen in the daytime come back to you in the evening when you're sitting and hoping the time will go by, so you can leave the warehouse and come home.

"There will be times, though, when I get angry at people. They just don't know how to manage their affairs, that's the trouble. They spend all they earn. They want more than they can afford. They forget how to shop; instead, they just buy what's easiest to buy. You can't have everything in this world. In this country we live better than they do in any other country! The average American has everything you really need to live a comfortable and happy life: good food, enough clothes, a warm house and all the electrical appliances, and a car. Sure you want more, but you have to pace yourself, and people don't, and then they complain about the banks and the interest rate and inflation and the government and all that. I don't say anything. I hear them out. I can't say anything. I'm there to keep nodding and try to arrange whatever I can that will help them. But a day doesn't go by that I don't want to shake somebody and tell them that America was built by people who knew how to make sacrifices. Today, everybody wants what he can get, and then he wants more, and he's never satisfied, and that's what keeps the whole country going, I'm afraid: people thinking they have to *have* things, and coming to us for the money, and then sweating themselves into an early grave paying us back."

Perhaps he is exaggerating. He knows he might do that, inflate and distort a little because he is so obviously "on the firing line," there in the bank. And he also knows that he sees things differently on various days, even from hour to hour. One minute he will be the stern, Yankee banker, full of epigrammatic advice about borrowing and lending and conserving and wasting; the next he will be the very salesman he detests — as he tries to get people to take risks, obligate themselves further, "live" while they can. As a result, his wife and daughter note the contradictions, smile at them, or argue with him. Moreover, he argues with himself, tries hard to reconcile the various viewpoints he expresses — or heard expressed by his father or his uncle or neighbors when he was a child. And maybe one day the psychiatrists that he mentions as potentially able to learn a few things by sitting near him and paying attention to the words he hears might also discover that severe "unconscious conflict" can be caused by political or economic stresses as well as by "family interactions" or "interpersonal relationships." Here, for example, is a man talking about his father: "When I think about my father, it's him struggling to pay the bills that I think about. He was always telling us that, how hard it was to pay those bills. He loved this country, but sometimes he hated it. I don't mean he was unpatriotic. No sir, he would have gone to war and given his life for America. He wasn't like these noisy college students, always trying to get out of their responsibilities, always making noise and telling everyone what they should think and do. It's just that the strain on him of the depression went to his mind, and he'd lose his control. He'd go to pieces, that's what. He'd wake up in the middle of the night screaming, and he'd say the next morning that the bills were like a noose around his neck and he was choking to death. He'd shout and scream at the rich people, 'selfish' he'd call them; and then he'd repeat it three or four times, selfish, selfish, selfish. Sometimes I'll be busy at work, and my father and his ideas will be the furthest thing from my mind, but suddenly I'll hear him saying 'selfish,' a word like that.

"We go to meetings with the trustees of the bank, and they're a rich bunch. All they want is more money for themselves. They shout at the labor unions for driving up prices, but no labor union can keep up with a bank or a big corporation when it comes to making money. Then, we go to church every Sunday, and the minister will read something that Christ said, and suddenly I'll hear my father again, talking about how 'selfish' people are. Christ knew the rich; he really did. He knew that the more they get, the rich, the more they want. And they can pick up their phone and get their Congressman to listen to them. And the newspapers and television stations, who owns *them,* the ordinary man? They say everyone's entitled to his opinion, but if you own a paper, you sure have more 'freedom of expression' than others do!

"My father would stop himself after a while and he'd reverse his direction. Do you know how? He'd start blaming the people for putting up with what they do. When he started saying that ('people get what they deserve') I'd know that he would begin to sound completely different in another minute or two. He'd say that if people wanted a better country, they'd have one; instead, they let the powerful people run the show, and the ordinary man usually doesn't care, one way or the other, what happens. He'd say that people, most people, have no minds of their own; they just go and do what they think they have to do, and they don't stop and think and try to change things. Well, my uncle once told us that my father was crazy about his politics; one minute he'd sound like a Communist and the next people would say he spoke like 'the spitting image of J. P. Morgan.' My uncle was older than my father, and he tried to help out when my mother took sick. But he had no money, either. He was an electrician, and all during the depression he couldn't find a job. He'd laugh and tell us that he couldn't understand how America had any lights at all, because every electrician he knew was out of work.

"I'll be at work, like I said, and I'll hear my father or my uncle. I guess my mind gets smart and puts them on a scale to balance each other. If my father's voice takes after the directors of the bank for being selfish, or the people who come to get a loan for being dumb, I can always turn to my uncle, because he'd say that things get bad, then they get better, and that's the way it goes, and you can't get carried away, you just have to do the best you can, and if everyone did that, the best he could, the country would be better off. I say that to myself all the time. Only it sounds better when it's my uncle saying it; maybe that's why I hear his voice speaking the words. You know what? Sometimes I'm not sure I really believe that, what he'd say back then. But what *can* you believe these days? The less you let yourself think about some of these things, the better. Sometimes people want to talk politics with me, and I won't let them. You only make a lot of enemies that way."

V

MANY OF THAT BANK OFFICER'S FELLOW CITIZENS certainly agree with what he says about politics. Several miles from his home a gas station owner says exactly the same thing, just a little more briefly: "To hell with politics; politics makes for trouble." Not that he doesn't hear people say what they think all day long; they come and buy his gas, and "before you know it" they're "sounding off." He arrives at the station early, around seven; he leaves the station around seven at night. For twelve hours he "catches them," which means he fills up one gas tank after another. One stands beside him in front of his station and does indeed begin to understand why he speaks of "catching" cars and "pulling them in." Wave after wave of automobiles go past his station, located on a moderately busy road, and as they come near there is always the question: will one or two stop and fill up, or will they all go by? Sometimes more than one or two stop, and the very limited area around the pumps becomes crowded with cars and impatient drivers who race their motors and frown and look at their watches and inch up close to each other, as if somehow things will go faster if all the cars virtually touch.

When the owner of the station hears *that* clever little observation he has one big laugh for himself — and comes up with a psychological interpretation far more to the point of it all, and far more in keeping with the kind of world both Marx and Freud, among others, insisted upon describing so closely: "No sir, they're not wishing time away. I think they'd like to push each other onto the road, so they'd get the fast service they want. In this world, everyone wants to push everyone else. It's amazing people *ever* put their feet on the brakes in time."

He subscribes to what he calls "the jungle theory" of human nature. People, to his way of thinking, "want everything they can get" and "take what they can." He lives within the geographical limits of a large city, but his customers by and large live in small towns, and are well-to-do, white commuters who drive toward the city and away from it, day after day. They seem to have everything he wants, but they are not happy, he feels, "mostly because as much as they have, they're not satisfied." He will make it quite clear that they *ought* to be satisfied; and as for him and his family, *they* are satisfied. True, he works long hours; and true he is on his own, with no guarantee that he will make anything at all each week. Still, he claims to

95

be content with things as they are. Let others make a lot of money working for a company or a law firm. Let them go on the road trying to sell things on commission. All those people have to report back to someone, have to take orders. So do workers, millions upon millions of them. They may have the unions behind them, and they may make a good week's wage, but "up above" are foremen and more foremen, and supervisors and superintendents and company officers and on and on.

Once he worked like that, "under ten people's noses." Once he was watched. Once he had to check in and check out. Once his every move was subject to argument and criticism. When he gets tired and angry he makes it a point to recall those times, those years, those moments; and all of a sudden, almost like a miracle, he feels better, easier about things, happier, and more determined to stay where he is for the rest of his life: "Look, I'll never be rich. I'll never be poor, either — I hope. Sure, sometimes I think I'm poor right now. The cars haven't been coming my way like they should. They're stopping up the road or down the road, or I begin to think they are. So, I say to myself that I'm on the way to bankruptcy. But it's never happened.

"I've had this station for seven years; that's a long time. I got it just before John Kennedy was killed. The poor guy. He was just getting going. He was a good man. He was on the side of the average man. So was his brother. He's gone, too — Robert Kennedy. What a tough guy he was. He could give it back; he was a fighter. I liked Ike, too. I wasn't old enough to vote for him, but my father did, the first time he ever voted Republican. I don't care much for either party. They're all crooks, you know. I vote for the man. Johnson was a crook. You could tell it on his face. I don't care how much he tried to do for the poor. He was a crook. Nixon is an honest man. He admits his mistakes; I like that about a politician. He's on the side of the big guys, though. You can tell. Humphrey — I voted for him, but I don't like him. My wife said he had a silly smile on his face all the time, and she was right. I would vote for Nixon today against Humphrey. Wallace speaks a lot of the truth, and no one else dares to do the same. Wallace isn't afraid of anyone. He'll never get elected; he's too straight from the shoulder. He says what a lot of us believe. I'll be honest with you, it's not easy to say certain things, especially in front of the snobs that stop here for gas. I hear them talking. They've got it made, and they're always sympathizing and worrying about the 'poor.' Hell, compared to them, I'm so damn poor it isn't funny. But let the price of gas go up, or a can of oil, and they scream at you. They've suddenly lost all their pity for people — for me, at least! Sometimes I think the way to get their sympathy is color your skin brown.

"And their kids! You should see some of the kids that drive in here. I don't know what they are, men or women or something in between. They're full of a lot of crazy talk. They look crazy. They act crazy. The trouble is they've never done a day's work in their lives. If I had a million dollars I'd make my kids work. And I wouldn't give them all those cars and fancy, crazy clothes, and the spending money. I think they're all on drugs. I don't know what they take, but it's not just a few beers. They act strange, real queer-like. They stare at you, and shrug their shoulders and have that goddamned silly, stupid look on their faces. Boy, I'd like to call the cops. Would I! But I can't. I'd lose all my business for reporting them. The parents would stop coming here. So, I shut my mouth and try to smile at them. I tell them to go you know where under my breath; I have to, or I'd blow a fuse in my brain. After I've had a few of them here — they come inside and want to use the candy machine, like babies they are — I begin to wonder if this country will make it, I really do! My wife says we will, but I guess women have to be more optimistic than men. The kids ask all those questions, and the mothers have to supply the answers and let the kids know the world will be around long enough for them to have a life for themselves.

"My wife and I, we agree on everything. We do. But she tells me to shut up sometimes, and I tell her to shut up other times. She says she agrees with Wallace, but she doesn't want our kids talking like him. I tell her she's got big fancy ideas in her head for them. She asks me what *I* want for them. Well, she's got a point. I wouldn't mind seeing my boys make more money than me, and have a good, safe job — so long as no one's on their back all day long. But if they get up there, and then their kids become hippies and nigger-crazy, then I'll tell you this, to hell with that! My wife and I sure agree on that. She says you can make money and keep your values. I hope so. Actually, I know you can. But it can go to your head, the education and the money. You've got to watch out. I think it's there that the mother counts. I see the mothers of these hippie college kids, and once you talk with them a few minutes you understand everything. They're not real mothers. They're women who have kids and then dump them on one maid after another. They're full of it, full of shit. They talk with potatoes in their mouths. They're running from society meeting to society meeting, or they're going to some museum to paint or something, or they're rushing to teach the nigger-kids. One of them told me how she goes to read to them, and how 'it makes a difference.' If she came near my kids, I'd have my rifle out, pointed at her. There are some real nice ladies that come here, too — but they're quiet, not always showing off, letting the world know who they're voting for and what they believe in and all the rest.

"I guess the world is made up of your good ones and your bad ones, and no matter where you live and how much money you've got, there's a mixture of both. It's the women who make the difference, between good and bad, so far as the kids go; I believe that. I think one reason I can work my twelve or thirteen hours every day is because I know that at home my wife is there, and she's a real peach. She's a good mother and a good wife.

A man needs that, and you can't buy it; you've either got her or you haven't."

Eventually, millions and millions of men come to that moment; they have had their political say, said a lot of what they believe, and then are moved to talk about what that gas station owner calls "the really important things" — their home life, their wives and children, their hopes and fears as husbands and fathers as well as workers and citizens. Not that the mind makes such clear-cut distinctions. Men carry their home life with them to work, even to the voting poll; and mothers — yes, as they go about being mothers — all the time feel the influence of their nation's traditions and values, its social and economic policies.

To be a gas station owner is to get up at five-thirty in the morning and shave and put on a work shirt and khaki pants or dungarees and put coffee in an electric coffee maker and put on the radio less for music and news than the weather, because the weather determines the road traffic and sets the day's pattern. To be a gas station owner is to leave the house while others are asleep and come home when they have already eaten supper — and do so day after day, except for Sunday. Lunch is a sandwich and coffee at a nearby road stand. Lunch is a laugh or two with truck drivers and waitresses. Lunch is a half hour away from cars, the highway's roar, and those pumps, ringing all day, registering sales, bringing in money "for me and for Shell, more for them than me, but enough for me to keep us fed, keep us afloat."

His wife buys the food, makes sure that the home runs smoothly. If he keeps them afloat, she keeps them swimming. And like him, she does indeed use imagery that has to do with water, with struggling for air, for survival: "We're not out in the West, fighting with the Indians, so it could be worse. I see those cowboy programs, because my kids watch them, and I'll wonder to myself if I'd rather be in a covered wagon, going to California, or here, worrying if I can afford meat more than twice a week, and feeling bad that I give my husband so much rice and spaghetti, and he works so hard. There are days when I believe we're going to go under, just drown. But you keep going, and the weather clears. I know we're in pretty good shape, compared to others all over the world, but you can't think that way all the time, the way the priest tells you; it's all right for *him*, the Church pays his bills. If he could see what we have to go through, the juggling of bills, to keep us afloat, he'd be a little more understanding. And then you read about the people on welfare who want everything for nothing. They actually believe they're entitled to the world, on a silver platter, while people like us work ourselves into an early grave just trying to keep even with things — and keep our self-respect, I'll tell you!"

She does indeed have her self-respect. She is a competent, hardworking mother of four children, who range in age from eleven to three. She feels bad that she does not get up with her husband, get the coffee going

for him, make him a big breakfast, but he will have no part of that: she is on the go all day, and he won't have her up so early. In fact she wakes up when he wakes up, talks with him as he shaves, and the night before has arranged things so that "all he has to do is put the plug in to have his coffee on the way." While he drinks his coffee and anticipates his working day by catching the weather forecast and thinking about the "oil and grease" jobs he has ahead, she also thinks ahead: "It's the only time I really do have to myself. Usually the kids are still asleep, unless one of them is sick or something. In between listening to my husband drink his coffee and listening to the radio, I ask myself if there's something special about the day, something I should be remembering. I try to keep the house on a schedule, so the children know they do things the same each day, and so I remember, too. I'm a great believer in order."

She is indeed; she keeps "a shipshape house." She is up at "six-fifteen or so" and soon dressed and "ready to go." Immediately she has her cup of coffee and cleans away "his big cup, all empty." There will be dishes to do throughout the day, because she believes in "keeping on top of them" by washing and drying them as they come, rather than once or twice a day. She would, of course, like to have a dishwasher, but they are too expensive to buy, cost money to install, and waste hot water, or so she firmly believes. Nevertheless, they are desirable, and maybe the day will come when they will be within the reach of the "ordinary person," which is how she and her husband and their neighbors refer to themselves. By seven o'clock what she calls "the merry-go-round" has begun and she is with her children, telling them what to wear, helping them dress, getting their breakfast ready, seeing that they eat enough, preparing lunches for them, sending three of them off on the bus. Then, there is the house to clean, her fourth child to feed again, her ailing mother to visit, her neighbors to "chew the fat with" in between various chores, the shopping to do, a "serial or two" that she "can't help watching," and soon enough the children to receive back from school, their supper to make while they play outside, their bedtime to prepare for, and finally, her husband's return home to celebrate.

She really does celebrate his return home. He is tired, but glad to be home, and she is tired (the kids go to bed early) and glad to see him. They have their arguments and disagreements but "it's a good marriage" she says, and he agrees with her. Sometimes, when she is a little bitter, she says that she and her husband haven't got the time or money for anything *but* a good marriage! And what does make her bitter? What causes her to complain, when she believes in not complaining, to become angrily outspoken, when she believes in keeping busy and quiet, to talk about social or political issues when she doesn't ordinarily pay them any mind or attention, and indeed considers it a waste of time even to vote — though she does, at least in those years a president is being elected? Rather obviously the answers can be listed: inflation, the war, the race and welfare problems.

99

Listen to her long enough, read between the lines of her remarks, and one sees those subjects coming up; and so one is tempted to say that because they are mentioned (though only occasionally) they are sources of her distress, the explanation for her outbursts, her spells of sarcasm.

Unquestionably she resents rising prices, and what they mean to a housewife with a set and severely limited amount of cash to spend. Unquestionably the war means something to her: she has lost a nephew in it, her older brother's "young boy." As for the blacks of this country, to her they are getting away with something; that is a plain and simple fact. They have the support of rich and powerful people, especially "that college crowd" and what she lumps together in the words "fancy suburbia," which means a suburbia beyond *her* suburbia, with its ranch houses, one beside the other, on quarter-acre lots, row after row, street after street, mile and mile, to the point that one remembers how to get to a particular house this way: take the fourth right after the shopping center, then the third left, then the second right, then the first left, then count five houses on the right. ("I have to be careful *myself*, you know; one wrong turn and I'm lost. The houses were all built by the same company.") And then, they get not only support and advocacy, those blacks, but most enraging, they get welfare: "Can you imagine that, they loaf around, and the taxpayer has to support them, while the rest of us work. Whoever heard of that! And their husbands sneak in and out, so the women are eligible for welfare. It's a disgrace!"

Yet, those remarks are, relatively speaking, rare and not completely representative. Moreover, it is all too easy these days for an observer to latch on to such expressions of disapproval, dismay, disappointment, resentment, whatever. And the people who are asked questions, polled, prodded by this or that observer (not to mention political leader) often enough know what to say, have learned their cues from the newspaper, the radio, the television set. They know, that is, as American men and women alive in the last third of the twentieth century, about the various difficulties their nation faces and they know that like everyone else they are supposed to belong to one or another, maybe several, groups of people or categories of population. But they resent the efforts of others so to place them, locate them, define them, pin upon them various descriptive words. They resent being found wanting and lacking and beneath and under and "lower" and "small" and vulnerable and subject to this weakness, that "problem." They resent (it can be the words themselves or the smugness and condescension that goes with the words) being called *lower* middle class people or parts of a *backlash* or members of an *ethnic bloc* or the *hard-hat* ones or Catholic *working class* voters or *Bible-belt* fundamentalists or *small-town* people. They resent being classified as anything. They want to be known as individuals, as particular human beings. Or do they? Who is to speak for them after all? Who is their leader? Who *are* they?

One goes round and round with those questions, and gets not very far. From home to home there are variations in sentiment, differences in mood, shifts in attitudes or opinions. And very important, all is not quite what it seems to be — which is usually the case with every single one of us. The woman just quoted above, for instance, will say repeatedly what she is presented to the reader as saying, but there are other things she also says over the length of a day, a week, a month. Perhaps we do her an injustice by failing to indicate the range of her beliefs, the breadth of her assumptions, inclinations, impressions, dispositions. Perhaps we ought to learn what she values, wants, has and likes as much as what she misses, detests, resents, and in moments rails against — so mightily that one wonders how, in fact, it has come about that she and others very much like her have never, never once, ended up asserting publicly what can be so passionately felt and given utterance to. I remember the time I asked her just that! At the end of what she herself described as a "fit," an outpouring of anger unusual in its duration and intensity, I asked her why it is that the millions of Americans who have had enough of riots and enough of welfare programs directed at "lazy people" and enough of hippie youth with their drugs are as "silent" as some claim them to be. *She* is not silent, or at least for a half an hour had not been. Does she think others are like her, willing to "sound off" (as she describes it) on rare occasions, but by no means eager to translate privately held views into publicly aired convictions?

Well, yes; she does believe in keeping her thoughts to herself. But that only begins to tell her story. She has serious doubts that anything she says will be heard. ("There are deaf Americans as well as silent ones!") Nor does she feel herself to have the time needed or the desire to make herself heard. Nor would she know what to do, how to do it, were she indeed to have such time, such desire. Some people have other things on their minds, she pointedly observes, than politics and social protest. She has "other things" on her mind, things that mean more to her than the situations and conditions and circumstances she does now and then happen to mention and comment upon. And a sure way not to find out what those "other things" are, is to ask her for them, ask her to list them off. Hers is not a mind comfortable with lists and enumerations. She is likely to stop talking altogether when pressed for her precise "position" or "attitude" toward something. Or else, she comes up with a few words she has heard from someone else and *recognizes she has*. Others may quickly and firmly and knowingly refer to those words as the clichés that rattle around in her mind and constitute in their entirety its essence; but if so, if she is indeed dominated by the slippery and short-lived slogans of politicians and journalists, she is at least to be given credit for self-awareness, for knowing what her affliction is. ("I pick up ideas here and there, in the stores or watching television.") Or *is* it an affliction to want no part of political rhetoric, and so to use political rhetoric in order to be rid of it, which means use stock phrases in order to end thereby a discussion almost before it can be begun?

In any event, if she is asked about what she wants for her children, and it is about ten o'clock in the morning, and three of them are at school, and the fourth is with his aunt and grandmother, who live not far away, and if she for some reason feels expansive and talkative, then one can hear a little of her hopes, even as tucked in between them one comes across the gloomier side of her mind, the more sinister side, it can be said: "I'd like my kids to be good people, that's what. I tell them to play a fair game of baseball and basketball. I tell them to do the best they can in school. I tell them to be optimistic and be kind to people, *all* people — but fight for their rights. I'd like them to marry the right ones; marry someone who is honest and friendly and hardworking. The person you marry can make or break you. It's very important. More than anything else, you have to know how to work, and keep at it. No child of mine is going to be lazy. I won't let them be. If you let a child be lazy, you're practically killing him. How will he learn to make a living? That's the trouble today, a lot of people are lazy, and you know why, they're lazy because they've been *brought up* to be lazy. That's how I see it."

Does she mean any particular people? No, she does not. Does she mean black people? No, "many different kinds of people." But in fact she will now say what she has heard said, and she hopes in that way to end the uncomfortable discussion: "It's the ones on welfare and they're the colored mostly, right? And when people stop trying to pull themselves up, and when instead they take all they can get from the government, and when they get by rioting and stealing and demonstrating and demanding from other people what they can't con the rest of us into giving them — then that's wrong, and I'm against it." But what is she for? Again, one just doesn't ask; or better, one gradually learns not to ask, not to push her with an urgency, a hunger for precise formulations that is not familiar to her, and perhaps strikes her as at best humorous. She gets her ideas across, though; over the months she does. And as a matter of fact over the years one begins to admire her for her refusal to be glib, her unwillingness to pour out long and clever statements about her "views," as some call them. She has no views, or at least she doesn't like the word. "Hell, I don't know what my views are! I change my mind every other day, I really do."

She spoke those two sentences the very first time she was "interviewed," and eventually her visitor began to get the point. Nor was she being willful, coy, dishonest, taunting, sensitive, evasive, unfriendly. (On and on go the nervous, demanding observer's adjectives.) She was rather being herself. She was asking anyone who wanted some knowledge of her (and millions like her) to stop and wait and look and listen and most of all think about one fact that is for her unutterable, yet comes across in her manner, her way of doing things and talking and responding to others: that is, the fact of her own dignity, her humanity, hence her complexity. True, words like "dignity" and "humanity" are used piously and casually and uncrit-

102

ically. And no doubt about it, in the opinion of many people she and her husband and their neighbors are not the ones who have a claim to such words — all of which they in their own way realize full well: "There's no great reward in this life if you just go ahead and mind your business and keep your head above the water and keep on working away at your bills. The people who get patted on the back and told they're wonderful are the colored because they were treated so bad in the South. (My people were treated so bad in Italy they almost starved to death and they had to come all the way here, which they didn't want to do.) If you're a student at a fancy college, then anything you say, the television people are there to take it all down. They put those doped-up hippies and radicals on the screen every other night. Maybe it's our fault. We don't want the attention, the people in a town like this don't. All we want is to be left alone, to do our work. Maybe if we talked more, we'd get the attention. But who wants it? I want to have respect for myself. If others don't want to give me any respect, then that's no tough luck for me. They can all go to hell! I'm as much of a person as anybody, even if I don't talk a lot of big words, and ask for pity from everyone, or else shake my fists and say we should have a revolution.

"What bothers me and everyone I know is that we keep doing the best we can, but we're not sure others are doing the best *they* can. The automobile you buy today, for all the money it costs, there's always something wrong with it. Either the company tells you to bring it back for repairs, or you have to do it on your own. My husband says that everyone tries to cut corners — the big companies as much as anyone. They make things that they damn well know will only last a year or two. It's trash, but you pay a fortune for it. You buy a toaster, and the next thing you know, it's on the blink. You send it back, and then you're told they 'slipped up' on a few thousand — like they do with cars. Now you hear a lot of talk about pollution. I've always known about that. We have a river two miles from our house; seven years ago, when we first moved in, we went there on a picnic. What a joke! The river was coated with some chemical, and dirtier than any water I've ever seen. We heard that companies dump their waste in it. What could we do? You're finally hearing that they're going to stop that, the companies. I wonder, though. I really wonder. You have to keep after those companies all the time — because they're crooks. They're out for themselves. They don't care about you or me. In this country, like I say, it's everyone for himself and it's dog eat dog. I hate to think that each of my children will have to learn that, but they will. I wish it could be some other way. I wish we could live different.

"The colored people, I think they've got lost in the shuffle. They're different from us white people; I mean they look different, so everyone notices them, and it's hard for them. I'm against a lot of them, because I think they don't do enough for themselves, but I think they have a worse time than the rest of us, and no matter what they do, and no matter how good they'd be, there are a lot of people who wouldn't have them living nearby. Even my husband and my brother-in-law, and they're hard on colored people, say that they wouldn't want to be born with brown skin or black skin, because it's just too much for anyone to beat, even if he does work hard. I feel sorry for them; I really do. The trouble is, you'll just be getting ready to say how bad we've been to them, when you see them rioting, you know — or your friend has her pocketbook stolen by a colored kid, and you get fed up with them all over again. It's the same thing with college students. I wish my kids would go to college. That way they'd get better jobs; they wouldn't have to work twelve or fourteen hours a day like their father, and have to put up with all the customers he puts up with, always asking him to do things — do this, do that, do a miracle a minute. But if I thought my kids would ever grow up to be like those demonstrators and the hippies — never! I'd never let them go to college. I believe you don't just become like that, though. Those kids have been spoiled. They lived in homes where they were taught they can do what they please. You can see by the way they behave: they're all wrapped up in themselves, and no one has ever given them a whack and told them to shut up, sit down, get to work!

"I don't know what to tell my little boy. He's eight, and full of questions. The teacher says he's a smart one, and maybe he'll be the one to go to college. He wants to know why we do this, and why we do that. He says he'd like to be a mayor or a governor. Can you imagine that? I tell him he's crazy; that's a terrible job, and it's a lot of double-talk that they learn to speak.

"I hate going into town; I'm afraid all the way that I'll be robbed and beaten. Is that the way a person should feel — in *this country?* And whether you're downtown or out here in this neighborhood, you can't depend on anyone coming to help you. People ignore other people. It's a sign of what's happening — like I said, everyone for himself. The police don't really protect you. They try to, but their hands are tied. Every time they try to arrest a thug, there's someone crying that he was born good, and we should feel sorry for him. Who feels sorry for the people those criminals attack?

"I once thought I wouldn't mind marrying a cop or a fireman. I was a kid, you know, and I guess I liked their uniforms. It was silly. But my girl, she's only eleven, and she knows better. Isn't that something! It shows you how times change. The other day she told me that she feels sorry for her friend, Sheila. Sheila's father is a fireman, and her uncle is a policeman, and he was nearly killed by a sniper; they haven't found the man who did it. And the colored people and their white lawyers, they say it's the fault of the police in the first place, because no white man has a right to be in a colored neighborhood. Some of the colored people sent cards to him,

Sheila's uncle. *They* know that he was protecting them against some wise-guy kids. The kids broke into an apartment, and he caught them making off with a television set. He asked them to stop and they didn't answer. He fired a warning shot, and they kept on going. Imagine that! And the apartment they broke into was a colored lady's, of course.

"Now, the lawyers and the college students, every one of them white and loaded with money, I'm sure, say the police had no right to fire on the kids, or be there at all. That's what the sniper thought, too! My husband agrees, you know. He says they should pull out of every colored neighborhood in America, the police should. Let them kill one another off, if that's the way they want to do it. But I disagree. What about that poor old woman, that colored lady? There must be millions like her. I can't believe most of the colored are any different from us. They're being egged on by the radicals, those white kids. They're the worst. They come from rich families, and they pretend they're poor — but I'll bet they're not going hungry.

"Anyway, I didn't mean to get off the subject: Sheila says she'll never marry a fireman like her dad, and my girl agrees, and my husband says they're both right. The police and the firemen in this country have the worst time, worse than anyone else. They're the finest people we have, but they don't make the money they should, and they're insulted every day. What's the use of risking your life if you don't get any respect for it — and no thanks, and no appreciation? The same goes for all workingmen. Our next-door neighbor, he's a fireman; but he has two other jobs besides. He says they'd be starving to death if he didn't work as a carpenter, and help my husband out at the station during the busy hours. You know, sometimes I don't believe it's the same country it used to be. I'm thirty-two years old. That's not old. My sister is twenty-seven. She has two kids. We both agree that it's terrible, what our kids have to learn about America — that it's being destroyed year by year it seems."

What does she think is destroying America? What do her friends, Sheila's mother for instance, think is tearing the nation apart so? Rather obviously, as her preceding remarks amply demonstrate, there are the agitators of sorts, colored and white, and their overeager sympathizers among the well-to-do and "respectable" people whose gas tanks her husband fills every day. To her they have all suddenly appeared in recent years, out of nowhere it seems. There is no explaining them. They look so different. They act so different. They swear. They threaten people. Or if they are merely the "sympathizers," they have the most astonishing, vexing, maddening kind of selective sympathy or compassion. That is to say, they condone certain deeds when done by some, but take after the same behavior when it takes place in others. And besides, maybe they are *really* the "enemy": not the blacks or Chicanos or Indians, not even the radical college youth, but the "rich liberal sympathizers" out in those fine, enviably fine towns near our various cities. Are not those "liberals" the parents of the troublesome college students? Are not those "liberals" the ones who advocate "surrender" abroad and "revolution" at home? And "meanwhile they do all right for themselves." Their salaries are large. They are respected. They travel a lot. They dress well and eat out often. They tutor black children, march on Washington against our policy in Vietnam, denounce just about everyone in our government and everything going on in our society — and all the while live enormously comfortable and influential lives. They may have black maids. They may have foreign girls who work and work and work for them — for a relatively small wage indeed, because they wanted to get over to this country. They may even be associated with companies, institutions, firms that in one way or another are very much part of the "exploitation" they as individuals denounce and work against.

VI

IT IS IRONIC INDEED: some of the complaints that our radical youth level against "suburbanites" are the very complaints Sheila's mother and father have. And we had better say a little about Sheila's mother and father before we let them speak for themselves, because they are parents not only of an eleven-year-old girl but two sons, aged seventeen and nineteen. There was a third son, but he died in Vietnam. His body was brought home, and he was buried after a large and heartbreaking funeral, which I was invited to attend and did attend. I had known Ralph about a year before he was drafted, sent south, then west, then so far west that he was in the East, in the jungles of South Vietnam. He was an outgoing youth, tall and a bit husky and very direct in manner. He hoped someday to be an electrical engineer, but rather expected he would end up being an electrician — a union man, and therefore well paid. If that were to have happened, he would have believed that he was "on the way up."

As mentioned, the father is a fireman, but also a part-time carpenter. The father wishes he had "stuck with carpentry." But he didn't. He couldn't. Years ago there were fewer carpenters, less need for them; and it took time to be trained, to get into the union. One of his brothers was a fireman, and helped him get a job in the fire department. And years ago "the salary we got wasn't so bad." Indeed it was a reliable, regular salary, and had benefits attached to it; a retirement plan and a medical plan. So, Sheila's father chose to stay where he was. But it turns out that more than anyone else Sheila's mother was responsible for the decision, and to this day she feels haunted by the pressures she exerted on her husband. Now, even her son's death figures in her sense of what might have been "right" and what she did "wrong." Had she not insisted that her husband remain a fireman, he would have in time become a "union carpenter," made much more money, and been able to send Ralph to college — which would have meant a draft deferment for the young man. Ralph really did want to go to college, but there was no money for him to do so, and he was an average student, not "one of the real bright ones." Ralph had even told them, the last time he saw them, that when he got out of the army he would go to college. He had saved money. He would be eligible for benefits. He would be an electrical engineer after all. But now Ralph is gone, and his father has a tough time indeed keeping up with the bills — and in general life seems grim and sad and frustrating. And the mother grieves and blames herself.

Sheila tells her friends that her mother and father will never get over Ralph's death. She also says that when she grows up and has children, she will name her first son Ralph. She misses her oldest brother, and she worries about her other brothers, also older, also endangered: Ted is in the army, but "still in this country" and John graduates from high school in June of 1970, "and you know what that means, it means he'll soon be drafted." So, two American parents, owners of a home that has in it a refrigerator, a washing machine, a toaster, a waffle iron, a television set and a car, feel poor, feel lost, feel confused, feel cheated. Their son is a hero to them, but a hero in a war others decry, denounce, attempt to end not by winning it abroad but abandoning it here, through a decision on the part of the government. What are they to think, those parents? How are they to make sense of their son's sacrifice, and who in America is concerned with their doubts and misgivings, with their vague feeling that *they* are the real losers in America, the really ignored, abused, betrayed, cheated, exploited people? Who writes explanations of *their* problems, analyzes *their* plight, comes over to *them* with offers of help, with pledges of concern, in hopes of an alliance of some kind?

As if they want "help," though! Let others demand charity, fall back on the pity of those various groups who seem ever on the lookout for objects of pity! At this point the observer, no doubt like the reader, begins to wonder how one ever can get out of such a logical and emotional impasse: people want what they do not want, call out for aid which they cannot, for the life of them, accept, and in general have two minds, at the very least, about all sorts of things. (Not that anyone on this planet does not have his fair share of mixed feelings about one or another matter.) In time, though, one does begin to discuss things, and mention the more obvious inconsistencies we *all* have; and that kind of discussion in turn prompts Ralph's mother and father to point out the inconsistencies they have spotted in others, rather as we all do — notice ever so clearly the "problems" in those we study or call "patients" and then "treat," or observe or disagree with or struggle against. Shortly after Ralph's funeral his father wanted to talk about Ralph and his generation. Maybe it was the tragedy he was very much living with, or maybe it was the beer in him, or maybe it was two years of visits on my part finally arriving at some meaning. Whatever the explanation, the man had, as he himself put it afterwards, "a bellyful of words" he wanted to come forth with, and indeed he did in the course of a long evening: "How can a father ever get used to the fact that he's lost a son in a war, and it's a war that's got everyone confused? I'm sure the Communists are trying to take over another country, like they always do, but I can't figure out what we're doing: one minute we seem friendly with the Russians, and you read more and more Americans are going over there and visiting and all that, and the next minute they announce that a hundred more of our boys were killed — by guns made in Russia, I'm sure. What is an ordinary man like me supposed to believe? What is Ralph's mother supposed to believe? Mothers don't talk with people like men do; they sit and cry their hearts out and suffer by themselves.

"I'm bitter. You bet your goddamn dollar I'm bitter. It's people like us who give up our sons for the country. The business people, they run the country and make money from it. The college types, the professors, they go to Washington and tell the government what to do. Do this, they say; do that. But their sons, they don't end up in the swamps over there, in Vietnam. No sir. They're deferred, because they're in school. Or they get sent to safe places. Or they get out with all those letters they have from their doctors. Ralph told me. He told me what went on at his physical. He said most of the kids were from average homes; and the few rich kids there were, they all had big-deal letters saying they weren't eligible. They looked eligible to Ralph. Let's face it: if you have a lot of money, or if you have the right connections, you don't end up on a firing line in the jungle over there, not unless you *want* to. Ralph had no choice. He didn't want to die. He wanted to live. They just took him — to 'defend democracy,' that's what they keep on saying. Hell, I wonder. If I was a colored kid, they couldn't get me to go over there. I'd sooner go to prison. Let them 'defend democracy' right here at home. Those big-shot American officials ought to ride their military helicopters over their own country, and see the mess *it's in.*

"I shouldn't be talking like this; I know it. I'm strong for this country. It's the best country in the world. Where else could a guy like me, who didn't even finish high school, live the way I do? I'm not floating in cash; actually, every week we wonder if we'll make it to the next, the way prices are. But we're not starving to death, and we have a nice little house here. And I can say what I've just said. No one's carting me off to jail. I think they *should* take some of those draft-resister types and put them in jail. What right do they have to demoralize the country, when our boys are over there, overseas, fighting. Every night it seems they announce new deaths. More and more innocent kids are killed. For what? I ask you, for what? I watch the news every night. I see some of those faces, the people who decide things in Washington. They're full of talk and talk and more talk. They've got their ideas and their plans, more and more of them. The President, he has one man, I read someplace, sitting around all day making new plans for what we're supposed to do here, there and everywhere, all over the lousy, rotten world. There's plan A for this country and plan B for that one, in case they go against us, the different countries. Then we'll send our Ralphs over. The President's adviser, he's not going over there to fight. His big brain stays home, and the Ralphs of America — it's *the Ralphs of America* who pay every time. Do they pay!

"I heard one of the President's advisers on a program; he was being interviewed. That man was as cold as our freezer. He kept on spinning off numbers and more numbers and he had everything explained, and he was so damn sure of himself. My wife doesn't usually say anything (nothing!) about what she hears on the news. But suddenly she looked up from her sewing and said she was sure of one thing — 'that man doesn't have any trouble sleeping at night.' I asked her what she meant. (I knew!) She said that he was so wrapped up in his own big, fat brain that a boy like Ralph couldn't bother him, even if he saw him being killed right before his eyes.

"I think we ought to win that war or pull out. What the hell else should we do — sit and bleed ourselves to death, year after year? I hate those peace demonstrators. Why don't they go to Vietnam and demonstrate in front of the North Vietnamese? Why don't they tell Hanoi to change *their* objectives, and stop invading another country? When *they* kill people it's OK; when *we* do, it's 'brutality.' The whole thing is a mess. The sooner we get the hell out of there the better. But what bothers me about the peace crowd is that you can tell from their attitude, the way they look and what they say, that they don't really love this country. Some of them almost seem *glad* to have a chance to criticize us; it's as if they've been waiting for the moment! I'm no mind reader, but I talk with people every day, and I can tell what a person is getting at. A lot of the people they interview on television, they say they're against the war, but they keep knocking the country — knock, knock, knock. To hell with them! Let them get out, leave, if they don't like it here! My son didn't die so they can look filthy and talk filthy and insult everything we believe in and everyone in the country — me and my wife and people here on the street, and the next street, and all over. No sir; they can talk, but now they're marching all over, and dynamiting, and trying to destroy the country. What are we supposed to do? Let them go and do it, drive us all nuts, listening to them and worrying what they'll do next to disrupt the whole society?

"You know what gripes me more than anything else? It's the clergy, the priests and ministers, who get sucked into this radical business. Ever since I was a kid the church was quiet on all these things; they never shouted at you about how bad the country is, and we're murdering millions of the colored and we're murdering in Asia. All of a sudden they switch their line on us. I grew up hearing on Sunday this was a great country; and now I get a sermon that makes me think I'm living in one of the worst countries in the world. Now, what in hell is a guy supposed to make of all this? I ask you? What do some of those priests and their minister friends think we are, light switches, that you can turn on and off, just because they decide to? It takes a man time to figure out what's going on. And who has that time? A man like me, who's working all day and half the night? Hell, I *dream* about my work, the jobs I have coming up and how much money I'll be making next week. The other night my wife woke me up. She said I was shouting so loud she was afraid I'd wake up the kids and scare them. She said I was dreaming. I said I couldn't remember. But in the morning, when I was shaving I suddenly did. I was in the supermarket and I put all the stuff on the counter, and the girl added it up and I didn't have enough money to pay. Then she told me to put everything back on the shelves, and I said no, I couldn't because we'd all starve to death. Then Ralph came into the store and he said if he could get killed like he did, then the store could forget about the extra couple of dollars — and they did, I think. The last thing I remember, I was still arguing with them, the manager and the checker, but they were nodding at me while I gave it to them. I must have been shouting. That's when my wife woke me up."

What does he make of the dream? What does his wife think — about the dream and his interpretation of it? One need not ask such questions. And really, why should one even care to ask, when the answers are both forthcoming and obvious? At least both he and she feel the answers are obvious and say they are obvious, say so repeatedly. The bills grow and grow, work their way through various "layers" or "levels" of the mind, and eventually cause nightmares of sorts. But Ralph, what of him? Why is he in that dream? Obviously he is there to justify a man's claim before his potential adversaries. Yet, there is something else to be said — by Ralph's mother: "I think my husband and I can't help but thinking that our son gave his life for nothing, nothing at all. I'll be walking down the street and I'll catch myself thinking that. I try to put the thought out of my mind, but it won't go away so easy. I have to find something to do, to get rid of the thought; that's the only way. My husband, he always says that what matters in this world is that you can pay your bills. Then you can look any man alive in the face, and not be ashamed. It's unlike him to want anything for nothing. That dream he had, and what he said about it, that's the first time in our marriage, over twenty years, that I've heard him talk about being entitled to anything that he can't pay for.

"We pay cash for everything, or if we charge, we never default on a bill. We don't buy if we figure we can't afford something. I think Ralph's death has undone him; more than me it's undone his father. He shouts sometimes that the peace people are so busy trying to feel sorry for Hanoi and for their people, and for the colored we have here at home, that they don't stop and think about us, all of us who have given our sons, lost our sons to the enemy. I told him I thought they want the war to end, so no more Ralphs will die, but he says no, they never stop and think about Ralph and his kind of people, and I'm inclined to agree. They *say* they do, but I listen to them, I watch them; since Ralph died I listen and I watch as carefully as I can. Their hearts are with other people, not their own American people, the ordinary kind of person in this country. I know when someone is worrying about me and my children, and when he *says* he is, but he's really elsewhere with his sympathy. Those people, a lot of them

133

are rich women from the suburbs, the rich suburbs. Those kids, they are in college. Those are the people who want us to surrender. They say they don't want more killing. They say they're worried about that place in Africa where they were starving, and Vietnam and the colored in the South. Do they ever stop and think what *we* think? They don't come out here and try to talk with us. They march over to the colored slums, or they demonstrate downtown or in the colleges. Are *they* America? I don't believe it. I'm against this war, too — the way a mother is, whose sons are in the army, who has lost a son fighting in it. The world hears those demonstrators making their noise. The world doesn't hear me, and it doesn't hear a single person I know. We have our ideas. My husband, that's what he meant with that dream of his. He was telling the people that run the supermarket to pay more attention to us, because when you lose your son, you deserve it. But I don't want anyone's attention. I want my son Ralph back. And I can't have him back."

The time is eleven o'clock in the evening; and even if it is a weekend evening, the time has come to go. Tears are too close at hand; and frustration and bitterness and a sense of futility — in speaker and listener alike. What is one to say? What is one to do? Recite one piety after another. Try to preach reason? Try to explain, expound, explicate? Insist upon this point or that one? Say no, no, it's all wrong, what has been said; instead, hear me and hear what my sensible, thoughtful, well-educated mind has to say? And one wonders precisely what a self-styled liberal, an ardent "dove," is supposed to say when a woman like that with devastating openness and simplicity mentions once again what others like her in their own way repeat and repeat: rich liberals have black servants who wait on them hand and foot, and not for all that much money; and rich liberals don't by and large lose their sons in a war; and rich liberals pick up one group, one cause, after another, so long as they can "pat the heads" of the people they support, and thereby assert for themselves, the generous ones, a certain power, a certain right of *noblesse oblige;* and rich liberals are a smug and arrogant lot, a self-centered and precious lot, a dogmatic and hypocritical lot, a noisy and wordy and in the clutch vituperative lot, as ready to kill off one another and spite one another as spare a distant African or Asian.

Rather than put things quite like that, she talks about "fancy, fast-talking students" or "the snobs who live out there" and how "full of themselves they are," and how much "they love to use the people they say they're helping," and how "gabby they are — gab, gab." And no doubt about it, a lot of what she says she has heard from others: friends, neighbors, relatives and also a whole range of newspaper reporters, columnists, editorial writers, and politicians. In a sense, then, she has been "brainwashed" — some of us would quickly say — and been made to think and believe all sorts of things that are against her own interests. Yet, who is to define "her own interests"? Inevitably we come back to that. Exactly which of us knows enough to speak for her, or for Ralph's brother, a private in the United States Army, or for Ralph's cousin, a young soldier, who also went to Vietnam but managed to survive, after several close calls, and came home and now builds, all the time builds, helps build a bigger, richer America.

VII

AT TWENTY-FIVE that cousin (Will he is called, to distinguish him from his father, Bill) feels quite able to speak for himself. He is married and the father of a little girl. He has gone abroad and fought and sustained a minor injury and come home and finished his training at a "technical school" and become a welder, which means he has joined the union, found the kind of work he likes doing, found plenty of that work to do, and found a place to live, a life ahead. He also is a "young American." He also stands on one side of some social critics' "generation gap." He also is disgusted with certain things. He is even "alienated." And his wife, his twenty-two-year-old wife, she is far from being "over thirty," far from being middle-aged and compromised by all sorts of social or political entanglements. Presumably she is one of the people some us claim we want to hear, want to turn toward — as we get more and more disenchanted with people who are defined by age, by occupation, by class and background as dishonest, as unbelievable, as hopelessly "behind the times," or "out of it," or corrupted and "co-opted." What "counterculture" does she belong to, then? What does she, a young American indeed, have to say about her nation's present "priorities"?

For one thing, she likes clothes, but cannot afford to buy them very often. She also likes furniture — modern furniture, smooth and linear and polished coffee tables and end tables — but she cannot afford to buy much of what she sees and likes. Not that her husband Will doesn't make good money. They are both pleased with his salary; but they have bought a house and the payments on it are high, very high, because of the interest rates; and consequently they will have to furnish the house (and buy clothes for themselves) very carefully and selectively. Will says this: "I make a lot of money, more than I ever dreamed as a kid. I work hard; and it's dangerous, way up there, putting a building's skeleton up. But I like the work. I really like what I do. A man can't be happier than having a job he likes. The real pain is Sunday, when we try to figure out where all that money goes. She's careful, my wife. She doesn't throw money around. But it goes as though there was a vacuum cleaner sucking up every penny we have. The insurance companies, they make a fortune on us. They charge huge rates for the car and the house, and they're always hiking the rates even higher. And the interest on the mortgage — I get sick when I see what we pay to that bank, that lousy bank. Food is high. Clothes are high. Every-

136

thing is high. You wonder who's *really* making money. Not me, guys like me barely get by.

"I'll tell you who's doing great: the banks and the insurance companies and the big companies. Leave it to them, they don't starve to death, no sir. They have their friends in Washington. When the squeeze goes on them, they pick up the phone and call the politicians, and soon they're getting help. A guy like me, he can't call anyone. If I pick up the phone, I find there's a busy signal, or the damn thing won't even work. Sometimes I really believe the only way you get listened to in this country is to have money, lots of it. They always tell you in school that this is a democracy, and every man has a vote, and every man is equal. But some are more equal than others. I read the papers. I read what those lobbyists do. Washington is covered with them, thousands of them, spending millions of dollars wining and dining the politicians, partying them, calling them and telling them all kinds of things, I'll bet. *We* pay for it; *they* deduct it on their taxes, the entertaining. A guy like me, I get my taxes deducted before I even get my check, and I'm lucky if I don't have to pay more in April! I tell my wife that it's too bad she doesn't work for a senator or something. Then I could take her out and chalk it up to my business. Maybe there is someone in Washington representing the welders, but I'll bet he can't compete with the insurance companies and telephone company and the big companies that are always trying to grab some land or some favor. Hell, who can keep up with them all — with their clever, crooked schemes!"

As for Will's young wife, she is pretty and quiet and utterly bored by subjects like politics or the war or racial conflict or even money. "I have to think about our money problems, but it's a pain. Most of the time I'm with my baby, or I'm on the phone with my friends, talking about *their* babies, or I ring up my mother; and there's Will's supper to cook. He loves his food, and he comes home ready to eat up the whole house. He works hard, and needs a lot of meat — and does it cost to buy it! I sympathize with the poor people. I wonder how they possibly can buy, if it's a strain even on us. It's no good to be poor. And the colored people, the Negroes, they have a real bad time. I wish it would get better for them."

She is by her own description "easygoing," and she wishes the country were less troubled, less torn by antagonisms and conflicts. She doesn't "pretend to know" what those conflicts are, nor does she know "what should be done." Most of the time she tries to forget — "forget the whole business, because it's just too much for me." Her friends, the "girls" her age, many of them now also married and mothers, share her lack of interest in social and political issues, her lack of enthusiasm for "a lot of talk." Where does talk lead to, she asks. What is the point of it all? She wants out of life essentially what she already has, and that is that. "I'm happy; I don't want a lot. I guess I'd like a little more money, so it wouldn't be so hard on us each week."

Once and only once she did add just the slightest reservation or modification to her description of her state of mind, her wishes for the future: "Maybe if I had more, if Will made more money, we'd soon be spending it, and then we'd *still* have the same trouble keeping up with the expenses." That was all she could or would say; but her husband was there and heard it and was prompted to speak, and what he said, what he on various occasions says, demonstrates how dangerous it is for anyone to make unqualified descriptions of what men like Will do and do not believe or favor or advocate: "She's got a point there. It's a rat race, it is: the more you make, the more you spend, the more you have to make. The whole economy depends on that. Mind you, I'm glad to be making the money, and I love the comforts we have. This house, we love it. We hope to stay here. We have four bedrooms, and we hope to fill them up! We decided to get a big house at the start, and leave it empty, until we can afford the furniture. It's better that way than moving from one place to another, as your family increases.

"I guess a lot of people never live the way we do. I'm lucky. My dad really made sure I stayed in school, and he helped me learn to be a welder — and he knew people in the union. As it was, I had to wait awhile. I'm against taking in people just because they're Negro, but I really feel sorry for them, the Negroes. They have two strikes against them. They're poor, most of them; and people, a lot of people, are prejudiced. I don't think a lot of my buddies are as prejudiced as they *sound*. I mean, I myself will say some things I probably should be ashamed of. But I don't mean to take an oath on everything I say! A lot of us would listen to George Wallace a while back and agree with him. Then we'd stop and think, and we'd decide he wasn't the man for us; he wasn't the kind of President we need. The one we wanted was killed: Robert Kennedy. I voted Democratic. I usually do. They're more for the workingman. You can't fool a workingman too long. Nixon isn't fooling me. He's an old Wall Street lawyer, right? Isn't that what he was?

"We argue during coffee break. One guy will say that Nixon is cracking down on the nigger-bums, and the welfare-bleeders, who cheat on the city and the state and loaf at our expense, the taxpayer's. But pretty soon the next guy will open up with a reminder that the Negro is only trying to get *his,* just like we tried to get *ours,* the workingman did. And who won't give anyone an extra dime, unless he's pushed? I'll tell you. It's the banker and the big businessman. And who is *their* candidate? And which is *their* party? Look, don't sell the American people down the drain. I mean, the ordinary workingman, he's not as dumb as some of those smart-assed politicians think he is. They try to scare us and throw us scraps here and there, but you don't have to be a college graduate and a lawyer to know who's for you and who is trying to use you. My dad never lets me forget what a struggle the workingman had in this country, to get the unions going. Now people say we're only out for ourselves and we're against the Negroes and all that. Well, I don't know. I've never been asked what I think in a poll, and no one I know has ever been asked. If they did come around and talk with us at work and ask us their questions, I'll bet we'd confuse them. One minute we'd sound like George Wallace, and the next we'd probably be called radicals or something.

"I can tell you something, though: don't count out the men in the labor unions, and a man like me, the ordinary worker. Like I say, we know a friend, a real friend; and we know a guy who's saying things we want to hear, but he's got his own reasons for talking like that, and the reasons are selfish. The head of our local said the other day that they're trying to split us up and get us talking against each other, the business interests are — the 'commercial interests,' my dad would call them. Well, we'll see if it works. I hope not. I'd like to see the poor get more. I'd like to see us push those doctors, so you don't go into poor debtor's court trying to pay your hospital bills and your doctor's bills. That's the biggest gripe I hear; I'm in good shape and I'm not old enough to appreciate how bad it can be, and my parents so far are in good shape, in good health, too. But everyone you talk with tells you that all you need is *one* illness in the family, *one* operation, and you've had it, you really have; you're wiped out, your savings are, and you're up to your ears in bills. That's why I'd never vote for Wallace or Nixon or Agnew or any of them. They're going to keep playing on us; that's what. Sure, I like them when they give it to those little bastards, the hippie students, and try to crack down on the mob element, and the people like that. But my vote goes to the men who are on my side, and I don't believe Agnew is going to do anything *real* for the workingmen of this country. You know what I heard a guy say? He said Agnew is like your favorite comedian: he says all the stuff you want to say, but you never do, not the way he can. But who's pulling the strings attached to Agnew? That's what he asked. You know his answer? Well, it was this: not the welders and carpenters and factory workers of this country. Agnew climbed his way up, and now he gets his damn fingernails manicured, I read, and he's a businessman, that's what he is — maybe the owner of one of those tight-assed banks that want seven and eight percent interest. Who the hell wants a man like that for President? You know, I hate snobs, but you've got to be honest and ask yourself if that man has what it takes up in the head to be President. I don't want a guy there just because he sounds like me shouting my head off over my lunch box.

"I mean, you have to stop and ask yourself what a guy is *for,* not only what he's *against.* I guess you first have to ask *yourself* what you're for and against. Most of the time I don't bother. I guess you do that when you go into the voting booth. Our next-door neighbor, he teaches in the high school, and he says that's what's so good about this country, that every man and woman can go and vote and make up his own mind. He makes up his — he goes all the time to the Rotary and the American Legion — and I make up mine. My dad wants me to join a club we have that's open only to people in the family. They call it the Cousins Club, and they meet once a week in a different home each time and play cards and talk and they serve good food, I've heard. But I don't feel old enough. It's for the older cousins and uncles and aunts.

"I guess you never know what people will decide until they go and vote and actually do decide. Even in the Rotary, even in our Cousins Club, from what I hear, there's a lot of talk; but you never can be sure what people believe, because they go changing from day to day, and they're not sure themselves. You know, when I hear somebody say 'I believe this' or 'I believe that' I say to myself: he believes a lot of things, and he's going to have to figure out what he believes *more* and what he believes *less*. My dad says President Roosevelt helped him and his buddies do that, but he says it's harder today to find a man like him. If you ask me, there's no one now a man can really look at and say, *he's my kind of man*. But maybe we'll get one later, when it's time for an election. I almost didn't vote in 1968, and I told my dad I might not vote again, ever again, if we don't get better people to vote for. And then he gets going on that Roosevelt, and I want him to shut up, because what's gone is gone. My wife is like him; mention President Kennedy and she's ready to start crying. Now, what the hell good does it do to turn your thoughts backward?"

His thoughts do upon occasion also go backward. That is to say, he can be nostalgic, too. He can wish for a more simple America, the kind he read about in school, and heard his mother (but not his father) describe. His mother was as hard pressed for money and as frightened as his father during the depression, but in his words, "My mother was at home, while it was my father who had to go and find work, and see how lousy the world can be." Nor are his longings *only* an indulgence in nostalgia. Again and again in the four years, now, that I have known him and his wife (which has meant seeing them when they were dating, then engaged, and finally married) his essential misgivings about and wishes for American society have come forth bluntly and often enough poignantly — in the form of questions at once naïve and utterly wise. Why can't people feel safe with one another, walking down a city's streets? Why do hospitals charge so much money, and insurance companies, too? Why do the towns and cities do such a poor job repairing roads, providing decent transportation, collecting garbage? What makes black people riot? What ails college students, the very people who seem to have so much, who have what men like him have always wanted and envied and still want — for their children if not for themselves? Why do people turn on their own country and support a nation we are fighting? What are we fighting *for*? And at home, what is going to be done to bring prices down, make the workers of the country feel safer, feel that they will be spared not only criminals and rioters but a depression, joblessness, hence a financial and personal disaster?

And beyond the questions are the affirmations; again, if they are partly indulgences of nostalgia, they are also deeply felt values put into words with conviction and concern. Will and his wife speak for no one but themselves, yet on the other hand they obviously share with millions of Americans more assumptions and habits than they or perhaps anyone — unless it be a novelist with the breadth and power of a Tolstoi or a Faulkner — can quite convey. Certainly I do not believe that the political and sociological and psychological categories which are meant to describe millions of Americans, perhaps a majority of the nation's citizens, quite do justice to the *lives* of those people. We all have a wide range of things on our minds. We all are pushed and tugged by various and often conflicting sentiments and desires and beliefs. And in so many of us there is something that defies words, that has to do with unstated intuitions or inclinations rather than proclaimed allegiances and preferences.

There are times when I sit with Will and his neighbor (Will the well-paid welder and his neighbor, a well-educated but not-so-well-paid high school teacher) and between the two of them feel I have before me millions and millions of Americans: neither poor nor rich, nor for that matter all that securely well-to-do; not blacks and not Indians and not Chicanos; not city dwellers and not completely rural people; not intellectuals and not professional men and not students and not business leaders. And as mentioned in the preface of this book, it may be easier to say who people like those two and their families and relatives and friends are *not*, rather than precisely who they are and what they hold dear and believe to be right and true and proper and desirable and essential. In desperation, though, one looks for themes, for patterns that appear and appear — maybe not so predictably, but at least often enough or consistently enough. So, it has come to mean something to me that Will and his neighbor and others I work with in neighborhoods like theirs like to go fishing and hunting when they can; like to watch baseball, football and basketball games when they can; like to drink beer and eat steaks and apple pie, if possible with a huge hunk of vanilla ice cream; like to give their wives a box of candy in the shape of a heart on Valentine's day, with the admonition not to get fat; like to hide eggs on Easter and buy many more toys and other presents on Christmas than they can possibly afford; like that feeling on Sunday of dressing in an utterly relaxed, casual and "messy" way; like suppers as early as possible; like coffee and donuts during work breaks; like bowling on a Saturday or a chance to wash the car and polish it up or wax it down; like pictures of themselves and their children and parents on their walls, or pictures of flowers or animals there; like to belong to a lodge, to a club or two; like movies, especially on television — "good, funny ones" or Westerns, or "detective stories" or "murder mysteries"; like songs like "America the Beautiful" and "God Bless America"; like music with melody to it, light music, fast music, slow music, swing music, country music, but not heavy music;

like cookouts; like a dinner at Howard Johnson's or some "good local place"; like a "fancier" restaurant every once in a while — but "not so fancy you can't swallow your food, and they're at you with wine lists, wanting you to go way over your budget." (And besides: "Who in the world likes a lot of that wine stuff with your food. Before a meal a beer or hard liquor is fine, or after you're through.")

One goes on and on, aware hopefully of the exceptions, the variations, the influence of a person's religion or occupation or age or ancestry upon his or her particular ways of living and attitudes and spoken and unspoken values. In one home Christ appears on the walls of several rooms in framed pictures — and liquor is never to be found. In another home there is no sign of Him, or the Bible; just a few issues of *Popular Mechanics* or *Sports Illustrated* or *Family Circle* or *House Beautiful* or *Reader's Digest* or *Time* or *Look* or *Life* or *Newsweek*. One family is young, likes Elvis Presley and Johnny Cash; another knows where to tune the radio for "the good old songs," for Nelson Eddy and Jeannette MacDonald, for "swing," for Glenn Miller's "Sunrise Serenade" (or "Moonlight Serenade") or Tommy Dorsey's "Lonesome Road" or Harry James doing (what language is it?) "Ciribiribin," or Benny Goodman saying with his clarinet, "Let's Dance," or crying with his clarinet, "Poor Butterfly." But whatever the music, one can reasonably often expect potato chips or popcorn, and good, meaty chocolates or assorted mints, and again, beer or ale, or as much coffee as one's stomach can welcome and accept. And whatever the religious faith, there is a sense of foreboding about the future based on the conviction that God's prescriptions (or merely the normal or tried and true or familiar customs) are somehow endangered — by individuals and groups and events that by now may have become all too apparent to the reader: long-haired, hippielike, sexually provocative and wanton and brazen and ambiguous students or "pseudostudents"; the colored, the Negroes, the niggers — and almost never, the blacks; the rich (often called "affluent") people (often called "types") who take up one cause after another, march here and there, distribute their largesse eagerly and conspicuously and generously, but always, it seems for others — in Asia, in the ghettoes, on campuses, on reservations, up mountain hollows or near farms that produce grapes.

And yet, for all those concerns and worries and outright resentments if not hates, there are other things going on in the minds of American farmers and American teachers, American factory workers and American bank tellers and American salesmen and American housewives. We who want to understand such people spend so much time trying to catch their words, their expressions pro and con on a variety of issues or problems. After a while, after the "relationship" has somehow, thank God, become established, after tense and guarded and wary moments have given way to more relaxed and open moments, after statements have been made, inclinations and impressions and predilections acknowledged and made clear, we retreat to our lairs, predators of sorts, to munch over the scraps and morsels we have persisted in getting. Meanwhile lives are lived, and the continuity of those lives is itself perhaps the most important "fact" any observer is left with — to think about and characterize as best he can. Nor do people talk and talk about those long stretches of their own existence — when they are working, eating, sleeping, making love, relaxing, going on visits, going for rides, playing games, watching games being played and yes, taking certain things for granted and assuming certain things. But what *do* they assume? If only we knew their assumptions, one says to oneself, *then,* then at last, we would know what they *really* believe, in contrast to what they *say* they believe in response to a leading question or an open-ended question or a series of questions.

I'm Tamie and I want to be a teacher because my mother wants me to be one.

I'm Roger and
I want to be a
sailor because I
can sink ships
and get a medal.

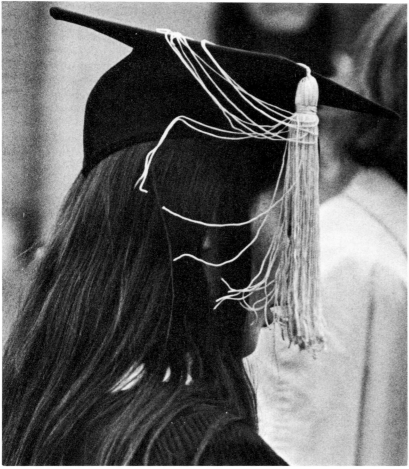

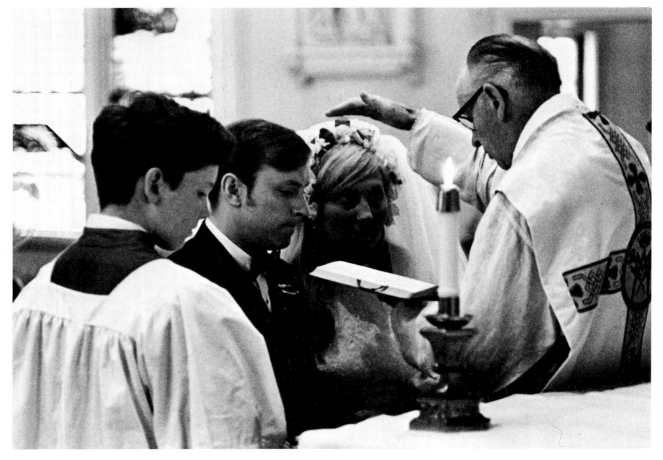

PHOTO OF STEVEN WEIGT TAKEN
IN VIET NAM. STEVE'S MOTHER
AND FATHER ARE DISPLAYING
THIS PHOTO THAT WAS RETURNED
TO THEM IN STEVE'S CAMERA.
MANY SAY THEY DO NOT KNOW
WHY WE ARE OVER IN VIET NAM.
STEVE'S MOTHER SAID "HE KNEW
WHY HE WAS THERE" AND THIS
PHOTO OF HIM AND THE CHILDREN
CONVEYS A LOT.

STEVEN WEIGT WAS THE FIRST
CLOVERDALE SERVICEMAN KILLED
IN VIET NAM.

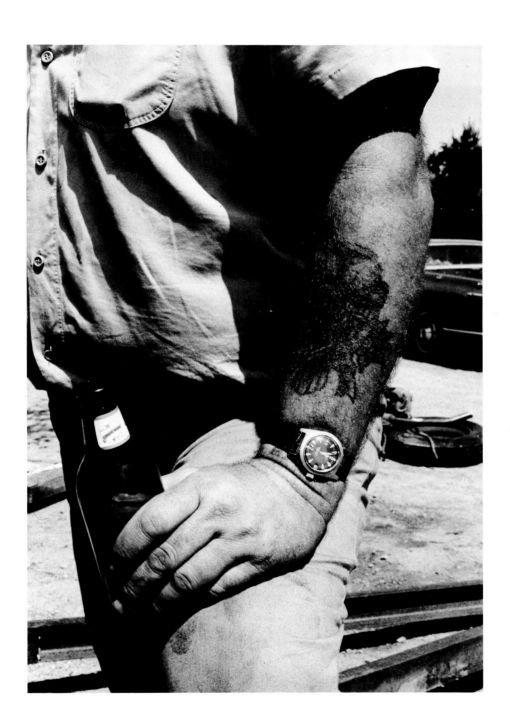

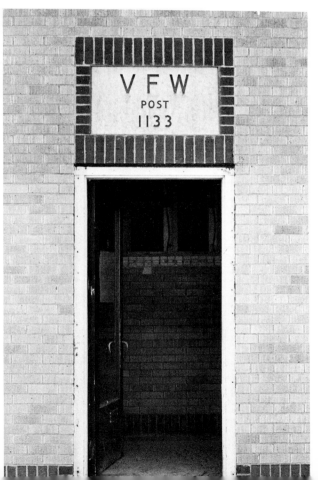

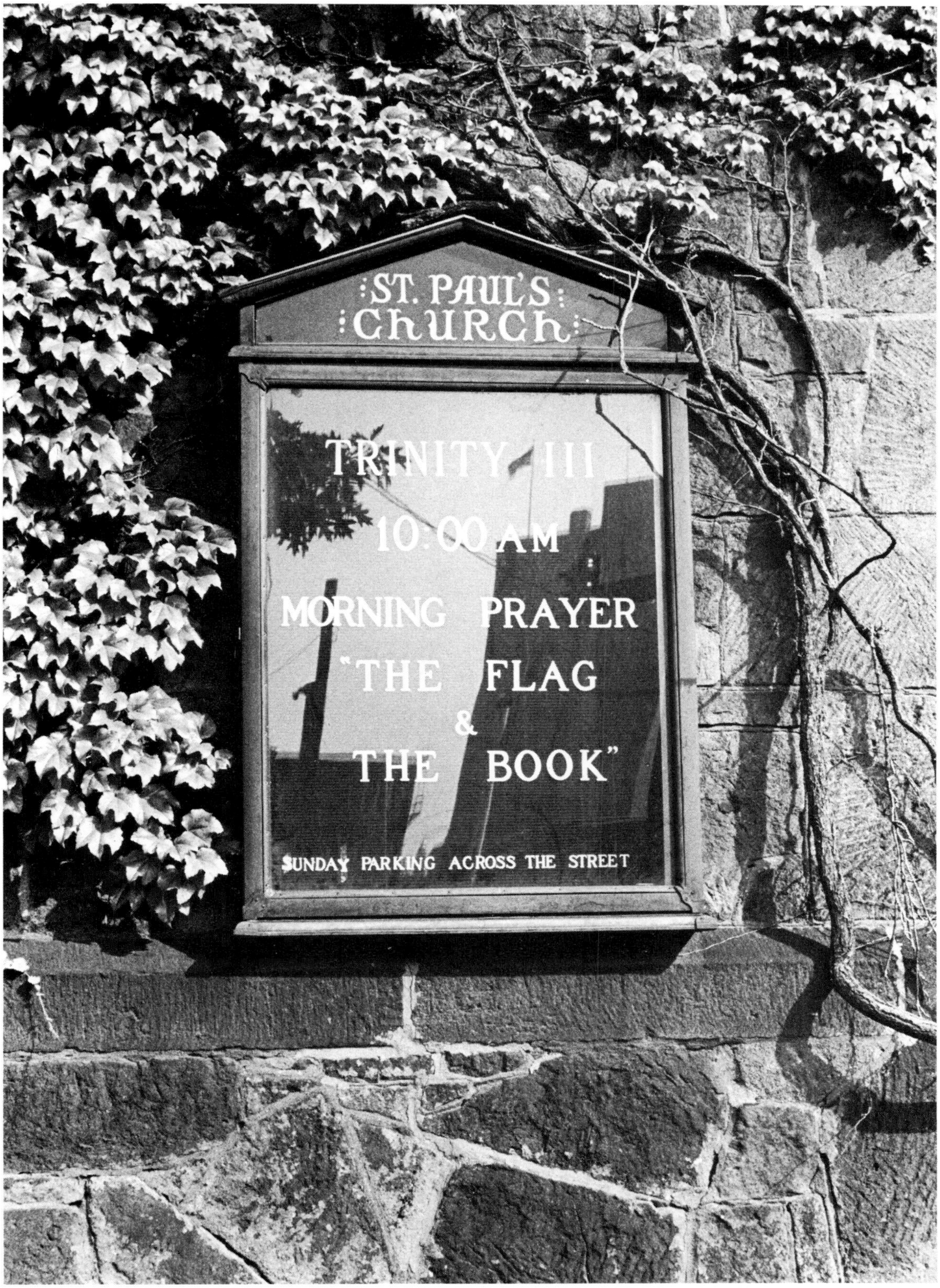

ST. PAUL'S
CHURCH
TRINITY III
10:00 AM
MORNING PRAYER
"THE FLAG
&
THE BOOK"
SUNDAY PARKING ACROSS THE STREET

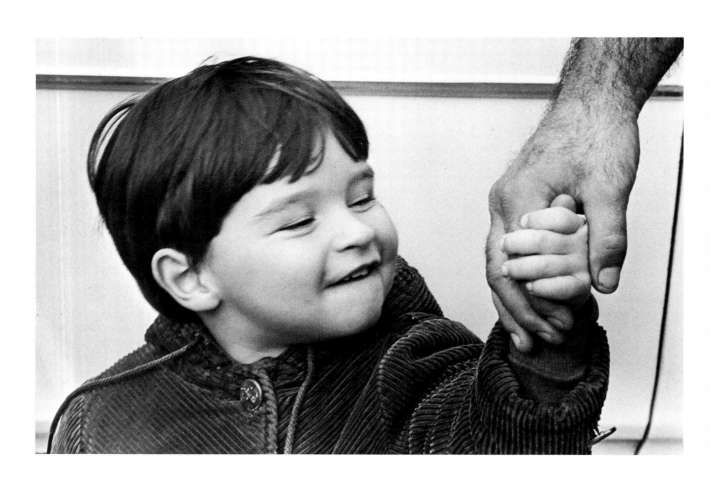

VIII

"I DON'T QUESTION MUCH, I have enough to do getting from sunrise to sunset." No, she is not "depressed" or "hostile" or overburdened or reluctant to cooperate or sullen. She is trying to be helpful, and merely reminding someone that it is easier said than done, easier to ask questions than find out what (if any) questions she asks herself *in the course of her everyday life*. And maybe her description of that life, that dawn to dusk schedule of hers, is the nearest she can ever come to talking about what she believes in her heart and in the back of her mind, way down there where investigators and interviewers and reporters and doctors and poll-taking, questionnaire-bearing visitors don't get to visit and poke around quite as conclusively as they, as we, might want to believe.

"I'm just a person," she once said. Then she added, "I'm just a mother." Then she added, "My husband is just a druggist." So it goes; one *just* follows another *just*. They are from the Midwest, originally. They have moved east because her husband's brother did so and the two brothers have always been close. Besides, in some farm communities "there's not much of a chance these days." But they have "family" back there, and they go visit them several times a year. It was the "service" really that did it, brought the brothers out of an isolated, rural setting and gave them training in electronics and made them in a way unable to return home. One brother still works in electronics, but the other had always wanted "to have himself a drug store" and by God, he has achieved his dream. He was "among the first to go to Vietnam," and he now considers himself "lucky" to have gone there when he did, to have survived, to have been able to go on and study pharmacology and graduate and find a store, a good store, to run. It was by accident that he found the store — "mere luck," his wife puts it. The store was owned by a druggist who had suffered a heart attack. The druggist's younger brother worked with her husband's brother in an electronics company. The brothers talked about the brothers, and eventually the drug-store owner left for Arizona and retirement, and his successor had a "long-term agreement" that enabled him to take over the store without investing a down payment, which he did not have.

One hears a lot about those facts, that story, the details and incidents which go to make it up. Indeed, one begins to realize, after a while, that what separates the druggist and his wife and brother and sister-in-law from the wealthy owners of drug companies or chains of drug stores is not necessarily a set of particular social or economic views, not even (always or necessarily) an "educational level," but a certain "tone" or "edge" to the concerns that dominate the conversations — and a tone or edge maybe best left to a housewife and mother (just!) to describe: "We feel as if we're more fortunate than we ever could have expected we'd be. Sometimes we'll both be up, and the children are asleep and Paul is getting dressed and so am I, and he'll look at me and say he can't figure out how we did it, but we did. And I'll agree. We've got plenty of bridges to cross, and it's hard, real hard, keeping out of the red these days, *but he has the store,* and for us that's a step we never could have planned and expected — well, planned, I guess, but not expected."

There just may be a lot to that distinction she made. Many men who belong to the so-called upper middle class, for all *their* uncertainties and worries and fears, can ordinarily *expect* a certain development in their "careers," and so their wives live accordingly, carry within themselves a whole set of assumptions based upon the likelihood that *this* will soon happen, and then *this,* and finally *that.* Not so with Paul and his wife, as his wife herself observes, among other things, in the following remarks, which are drawn from three separate talks, one of which she herself was moved to describe as "more philosophical" than is usually her custom to have: "My father had a small farm, and he lost it in 1938, after holding out through the worst of the depression. He went to work for another farmer who had more land. But he was never the same, my mother says. He seems all right to me. Even now that he's getting old he seems perky and happy to me, but my mother says I should have seen him when he was a boy, full of life and hope — and he was quite young, you know, when the farm failed. My husband's family was like ours, just plain people. They're not poor and they're not rich or important or like that. They're in the middle, I guess you could say if you wanted to put them someplace. His grandfather used to manage the railroad station in the town: sell tickets, keep it looking good, see that people got on and off safely. But now there's no railroad that goes through there. Paul's father was killed when Paul was eight. He worked in the hardware store. He used to tell Paul to be a doctor, Paul can remember, but Paul was lucky to finish high school. You have to have money to go on and on in school, or be smart enough for a scholarship, and even if Paul got one, he and his brother needed to make money to help his mother and his two younger sisters. Then they got drafted, the two boys, and that was what made the difference in their lives, they say.

"Sometimes I'll be dusting the living room or cooking and I'll say to myself, now how did you ever get here, and how did Paul ever get that store for his very own. It's like a dream come true; or rather, he's worked to make it come true. But a lot of people in this world work and work, they work all their lives almost like slaves, and still they don't get much, for all their work. They get nowhere, I guess. I don't mean to talk against people. It's just that one of my neighbors says that her husband is making a good salary, and she's glad; but the fact is he'll always be where he is now, taking orders all day long and afraid he'll be laid off as soon as there's the slightest trouble with the economy. By the way, that's the new word in my life, the 'economy.' Paul talks a lot about it, the economy. He says when you're trying to make your own business work, you have to think about *other* people's businesses, and how much money they're going to have for buying perfume and candy and watches, the things he sells in addition to drugs and — well, you know! — shaving cream or razor blades or toothpaste or the magazines.

"We don't really know much about the economy. We don't really follow the news that carefully. I'll be doing my work, changing Paul junior's diapers or washing the dishes and I'll hear the news, but when the music comes back, I'll suddenly realize that I've been listening to five minutes, *five minutes* of the news and I haven't heard a single word the man spoke, not a word. If you ask me what he said, I'd have to say nothing, nothing I can remember. Paul brings home the papers he doesn't sell, a copy of each one, and the same with the magazines; and neither of us look at them much. I like *Life* and *Look,* but it's the pictures, really, I confess. I don't much like those fashion magazines. They're too showy. They're for the rich. You have to be a dreamer, if you're in my shoes, to like those things. I guess I do my dreaming with the serials; the babies are asleep and I half doze and listen, or I go all the way and nap myself. Soon Betty will be three, and won't want to nap. The way she's acting now I can tell. Then I'll have to give up my own nap; unless I can get her to lie down with me and we would talk and tell stories to each other. I don't think she could follow the serials, though.

"To me the most important thing is that we're in good health, and Paul likes what he's doing. He gets nervous sometimes. He gets afraid we won't ever pay off the drugstore, so it's *really* ours. But I tell him I can't believe we'll ever go into the kind of slump I used to hear my dad talk about. That's what he used to call it, the 'biggest slump ever.' Paul and I think the country is too rich to let that happen; but who knows — not us I guess. I know there are a lot of troubles in the country, but for us, it doesn't seem half as bad as they say in the magazines or the papers. We'll be listening to the "Today" show, or Walter Cronkite, and we can't recognize America from what they tell you. The other day Paul said it wasn't *our* world, the one Cronkite talks about. Paul comes home and he's tired — the store opens at eight and closes at ten, and he comes home for an hour or so and watches the news and has supper and says good-night to the children. He has a fine young man helping him out. Paul says he goes back and the fellow asks him what's new in the world, and Paul says, 'Nothing, it's the same old world.' We honestly believe, we do, that they dig up a lot of things every day, the news people do, because they've *got* to; it's their bread and butter. Then we listen to it, or read it, all they've dug up, and we're supposed to go tearing our hair out.

"I'm not saying the world is just one big piece of apple pie. I know there's trouble all over. I feel sorry for the Negro race. I think it's hard, being them. I think we have got to finish that war in Vietnam, somehow. But this is the greatest country in the world, and I'm optimistic by nature. When I get up in the morning I say to myself that I'm going to try to do the very level best I can, so that Paul junior and Betty have a good day, and my husband comes home to a good supper, and I'm in a good mood for him, to help him relax, and the children are also in good spirits, so they can enjoy their father and he can enjoy them. On Sundays, thank God, the store is closed after eleven-thirty in the morning. Paul has to open for those few hours. It spoils the day, but he can't help it. A lot of business comes in during those few hours. People stop on their way to church, and even before then. They like to buy things on Sunday, it seems. I feel sorry for myself — that he's up and at work *every day of the week*, but we have a nice time on Sunday afternoons. We love to take the children for a walk. We both love to get dressed up then. And of course we visit Paul's brother, or they come here. It's nice to have them nearby. I couldn't imagine living without them. You need *some* family near you.

"I'd like Paul junior to be like his father — hardworking and honest. If he wants to go to college, that's fine. I'd like him to go. Paul says maybe his son will be a doctor. In America anyone can rise up and be important, so long as he works hard — and so long as he gets the breaks. Luck is important. But, if you're just sitting there, waiting for luck, waiting for the world to fall into your lap, then you're going to be waiting forever. Betty is a pretty girl, and I can tell even now that she's going to be a friendly person. She's very good with other children. So, we think she'll be fine. It's important to be able to get on with people, you know. Paul has to keep smiling all day long. It really makes a difference to the customers. He says that when he's feeling bad, with a cold or something, his business goes down that day. It just does. I used to think he was exaggerating. But I've been in the store, and I've seen how he really sells, oh does he, when he's in a good frame of mind and all smiles. He goes after the customers, and he tries to help them, and he reminds them of what they may want to buy, and he asks questions — whether they forgot this or that. He's not pushy. That's no good. He's the gentleman that he is, that's what; and then they go and buy a few extra things, and of course it helps them, because they don't have to make so many trips.

"Paul goes to the Rotary, and the Junior Chamber of Commerce. He likes the Rotary better. He doesn't feel he's a Chamber of Commerce type. A lot of them, they're too ambitious. They're working their way up in some company, the young men in the Chamber of Commerce. Paul wishes we had a 4-H Club here, but that's gone. That's not the kind of thing you'll find in a suburb or a city. He's waiting for Paul junior to become a cub scout and a regular scout. The happiest time he had in Indiana was with the scouts. The scouts were his life for a while. One branch of his family is out in Idaho, you know, and there's a distant cousin there who's very big in the scouts, and in the 4-H Club, and he owns land, a lot of it, and besides that he has an agency, a Chevrolet agency. 'He's into everything,' Paul's mother says. It's her aunt's son, I believe — Paul's second cousin. They are coming east next year, and they're supposed to visit us. We got a letter from them and they said it's the one and only time they plan to go east of the Mississippi for any length of time. They're happy where they are. You get to like the place that brings you happiness; that's my philosophy. If Paul was doing well with his drugstore and we were in Florida or California or Idaho or Indiana or Canada or Europe or the North Pole, or Alaska and places like that, I'd still be as happy as I am here. My sister-in-law says no. She says she can't stand very hot weather, and she's glad we don't live in the South; but I tell her, she'd change her mind if she *had* to, if her husband said, look: we've got to go there, if we're going to eat, and it's where I can work and bring home the bacon. She'd say yes, dear, it's up to you. What choice does a man's wife have?

"I have a neighbor who keeps on saying that no one has much choice anymore; that unless you have money, and you're a lawyer or own a big business, then you're just going to be pushed around and pushed around. She says she and her husband never vote, and they don't belong to anything, and all they do is try to save up enough money to go away on a vacation every year. We can't do that, not now, go on long vacations — not until the drugstore is *ours;* but I don't look at life the way my neighbor does. Sure we don't have much say these days about most things, but the average man and woman never did. My father and my grandfather used to talk the way I do, I know that. They were always adjusting themselves to the rising price of this and the price of something else, and my father says it was worse in America for the average man years ago than now; we have social security and the medical benefits for the older people and you can't overlook that.

"I'm optimistic, like I said. The American people are good people, I mean the plain old, ordinary, average American people. I think Paul and me, we're ordinary people, ordinary American people. We're not living high off the land. We're not picking up dollar bills that fall from some tree in our backyard. We've got our troubles now, and I do believe we'll have them until our last day here on this earth. But I can't picture myself living in any other country, no sir. Yes, I did say I'd move anywhere if my husband had to, but he never would. How *could* he? He loves this country, and so do I. We're not those professional patriot types. We don't believe that you follow the leader, even if he's dead wrong. We were all born Republicans, but we voted against Goldwater — and now I do believe that was a *mistake*. I think Johnson caused a lot of trouble for this country, the way he got us into that war. He was a sneak. You could see it on his face. But he sure fooled us in 1964. If your country has made a mistake, you've got to correct it. I hope President Nixon does, and I believe he will. He's a fair person. So is the Vice President. I think most Americans are. I liked John Kennedy. I would have voted for Nixon against him, like my dad did. But he said he would have voted for Kennedy the second time around. But we never did get a chance, did we?

"Politics — I don't have a mind for it. Neither does Paul. He reads the papers; and sometimes he'll mention something to me. We try to follow the important events. The customers talk about things to Paul, and then he brings home the news to me — what they say to him. There are more Democrats here than out in the West; farmers are suspicious of the Democrats, I think. We're not really devoted to either the Democratic or Republican parties. When someone asks Paul his party, he says, 'Neither, independent.' Why should he make an enemy of one or the other kind of customer? Most people, they don't really know what the difference is between the parties, anyway. I don't. I don't follow closely enough what they say, the politicians. I *do* believe that we have got to keep the crime rate from going up so high that we're all afraid to leave our homes. Paul says, just you wait and see, in a few years we'll get out of the war, and the country will settle down. He says the Negro people will be getting a better life, year by year, and then the country won't have the riots. I hope so. We're lucky out here; there are no Negro people and no slums, and so we have a quiet life. I'm not against anyone because of the way he looks, or she looks. I believe what I learned in school and in church, that everyone is created equal by God. How else would the Lord do it? He Himself was a persecuted man. I'll never forget it, when our minister told us that. The American people are not going to keep Negroes persecuted forever. There is a change in the way people think. My father says he used to say a lot of foolish things, *bad* things, about them, the Negroes, but now he doesn't, not the way he used to. He's never really had much to do with them, that's it. Now, he says, you see them all the time on television, and they're in the news, and you can't help but feeling the atmosphere is changing for them. They may want it to go faster, the change, and some people say we're going too fast (I hear that, 'too fast,' people say) but I think we're heading in the right direction, this country is.

"Sometimes when I have the television set on, and I hear people saying all those bad things about this country, the wrong we've done, they say, and how the American public, the people of this country, are prejudiced and they're turning against the poor and all that — well, I don't know who they've been talking with, because it's true that everyone likes to be with his own kind of people best of all, and maybe there *are* a lot of selfish people in this country, who don't remember what Christ said about the poor, and how He urged us not to fight and kill. But there are other people here, too; and I believe the majority, a big majority, of the American people are truly decent and God-fearing people. I don't like to compliment my own country, over other countries I mean, but I can't say it too often: I think we're all right, this country is. God will make the judgment, I guess. And the minister tells us that we have no right to speak for Him. While the children are small and my husband is working on Sunday mornings, I've had to stop going to church, except once a month or so, when my sister-in-law comes over and helps out. But even so, even if no one can read God's mind, I believe that God must have had a special place in His heart for this country.

"America is such a beautiful country. God has given us so much, so very much, and allowed us to prosper so. And we have tried to be good and helpful; we've helped so many other countries. So, if we're not perfect, then we're not bad, not as bad as you hear it said. And the most important possession we have is our people. Paul says that his average customer, he's a fair and square person. I think that's the case all over the country. If we keep having fair and square leaders, too, and they ask us to dig our heels in and work hard and solve our problems — well, I believe we will. I hope we do, so that my children won't be looking at their father and me and wondering what we were doing all those years while they were growing up. That would be terrible, if that was to happen, if the country was in a bad state, and our children decided we'd somehow failed them. But I don't feel that my parents failed me. They worked with all their might and did what they could for me and my sister and brother. And I hope I'll do the same, I do. That's my hope, my objective, I mean: to do what I can for my children so that they can do the same for their children. And isn't that what we're here for? If someone asked me what I believe in, that's what I'd answer him with. It may not be the smartest kind of philosophy, but it's what a mother ought to be saying to herself in her heart all the time."

She gives every indication of doing so herself: keeping in mind life's utterly rock-bottom essentials. Quiet, soft-spoken, shy and self-conscious, she can also be straightforward, talkative, a bit truculent, self-possessed and unashamedly outspoken. Once she called herself a "fighter." Once she said she might have a little "bigotry" in her. Once she said she wished she had gone beyond high school. Once she said she was glad that she wasn't "too filled up with a lot of knowledge," the kind that makes people self-important, prideful, too sure of themselves. Once she said she didn't want much out of life. Once she said she wanted so many things that she had to stop herself from thinking about them all, because there is a limit, an absolute limit, to the greed a person ought let himself reveal, even to himself. Once she essentially described her husband as a tough, able, shrewd businessman. Once she said that he was so soft, so generous, so concerned with people that "it's a wonder he charges them anything at all."

Rather obviously, she and her husband, as she has said, are *themselves,*

179

and ought not be anyone's means of denying them their individuality. I have not spent time with them these past years in order to bury them in one abstraction or generalization after another, until indeed they will disappear, the victims of enemies they, for all their sometime suspiciousness, never imagined around and waiting. But rather obviously she and her husband are to be taken at their word: they certainly do "resemble a lot of other people," and they certainly do have their ideas about not only themselves but their fellow citizens, and they certainly do deserve the respectful and thoughtful attention of those very political leaders they both tend to doubt ever give them "one blessed thought," except perhaps during election campaigns. Too much happens in between those campaigns for their occurrence every two or four years to be the occasion and measure of a nation's concern for its citizens.

And one more thing, this by way of a conclusion to the book. The woman and her husband just described and quoted actually "resemble" just about everyone in the United States in more ways than some of us may care to acknowledge. Politicians and social scientists have of late been almost desperately anxious to put a rope around people like that woman and her husband. They have been seized, as it were, pinned down and branded with all sorts of names — and at times it seems there is a name for their every value and belief and habit. In so doing millions and millions of people become "them," become one more "group" to be pitied or exploited or scorned or praised for a dozen obvious or not so obvious reasons. What the men and women in this book struggle with most of us struggle with; "they" in many respects are "us," are twentieth-century Americans. All of us are proud, are confused, are uncertain, are plagued by doubts and misgivings, feel moments (and longer spells) of bitterness, envy, spite. None of us really wants to be defined by sweeping psychological and sociological generalizations: you think this, you think that, you live here, you live there, hence you *are* one thing or something else.

I hope I have achieved in writing this book only the observer's distance and no more. Put differently, I hope I have shown how particular Americans contend with problems that plague just about all Americans. I am thankful that the photographs round out enormously the analysis this book attempts. We are reminded in looking at them that a person talking about himself often isolates himself, abstracts himself, abstains from mentioning so much that goes on about him, so much that happens. Once in the course of my work I heard these words: "I make things sound worse when I talk about them; and I make myself seem lonelier." That woman, that mother, that wife of a telephone repairman, that neighbor of someone quoted earlier in the book, had a lot to tell me — tell all psychiatrists.

If condescension is one risk a book like this faces, another is its avowed lack of sustained political analysis and social criticism. We have tried to convey what we have heard, show what we have seen; it is quite possible that our own insularity, parochialism, snobbery, and self-centeredness will come across to some readers in the way "we" talk about or picture "those people." By the same token, other readers will want more of "us" in this book — only they will have in mind a presentation of our views and attitudes, an analysis of "white racism" or "consumerism" or "the politics of fear" or the "insecurities" and "rigidities" and "acquisitiveness" of what one hears called by certain political theorists or historians "the petite bourgeoisie." Here I can only repeat what I have written in book after book, including two previous photographic texts aimed at bringing before readers the consequences of the life that goes on within the ghetto (*The Image Is You*) and the consequences of the hunger many Americans continue to endure (*Still Hungry In America*). That is to say, I can only emphasize my limitations. I try hard to know people, learn what they think, understand what they feel. I spend a long time trying to set all of that down as coherently and sensibly as I can. Books and books can no doubt be written about the various issues that the words and photographs on these pages suggest. I can only hope that the work Jon Erikson and I put into this book helps others write the additional books we all most assuredly need. But if Americans need more books I believe Americans also need a little more kindness toward one another, a little more of the charity Christ urged upon us. Those who write books, *we* who write books, are particularly apt to get swollen with ourselves — and so forget about our own sins and crimes and "problems" (as they are called in this day and age) ; hence, again, our need to struggle for the charity toward others we hope they will in turn offer back to us.